OECD
ECONOMIC SURVEYS

YUGOSLAVIA

ORGANISATION FOR ECONOMIC CO-OPERATION AND DEVELOPMENT

Pursuant to article 1 of the Convention signed in Paris on 14th December 1960, and which came into force on 30th September 1961, the Organisation for Economic Co-operation and Development (OECD) shall promote policies designed:

- to achieve the highest sustainable economic growth and employment and a rising standard of living in Member countries, while maintaining financial stability, and thus to contribute to the development of the world economy;
- to contribute to sound economic expansion in Member as well as non-member countries in the process of economic development; and
- to contribute to the expansion of world trade on a multilateral, non-discriminatory basis in accordance with international obligations.

The original Member countries of the OECD are Austria, Belgium, Canada, Denmark, France, the Federal Republic of Germany, Greece, Iceland, Ireland, Italy, Luxembourg, the Netherlands, Norway, Portugal, Spain, Sweden, Switzerland, Turkey, the United Kingdom and the United States. The following countries became Members subsequently through accession at the dates indicated hereafter: Japan (28th April 1964), Finland (28th January 1969), Australia (7th June 1971) and New Zealand (29th May 1973).

The Socialist Federal Republic of Yugoslavia takes part in some of the work of the OECD (agreement of 28th October 1961).

Publié également en français.

Table of contents

Tables

4

Diagrams

This Survey is based on the Secretariat's study prepared for the annual review of Yugoslavia by the Economic and Development Review Committee on 27th April 1990.

●

After revisions in the light of discussions during the review, final approval of the Survey for publication was given by the Committee on 22nd May 1990.

●

The previous survey of Yugoslavia was issued in July 1988.

BASIC STATISTICS OF YUGOSLAVIA

THE LAND AND THE PEOPLE

Total area (1 000 sq. km)	256	Net increase in population, 1971-1988 (1 000),	
Agricultural area (1 000 sq. km), 1986	142.0	annual average	179
Forest area (1 000 sq. km) 1986	93.0	Total paid employment (1988, 1 000)	6 715
Population (30.06.1988, 1 000)	23 556	*of which:*	
Republics:		Industry	2 716
Serbia	9 778	Building	554
Croatia	4 681	Agriculture (social sector)	245
Bosnia and Herzegovinia	4 443	Active population in private agriculture (1988, 1 000)	2 165
Macedonia	2 088		
Slovenia	1 943		
Montenegro	633		
Major cities (1981, 1 000):			
Belgrade	1 470		
Zagreb	856		
Skoplje	505		
Sarajevo	449		
Ljubljana	305		

PRODUCTION

Gross national product at factor cost		Origin of GDP in 1988 (per cent of GDP):	
(1988, billion dinars)	154 292.4	Agriculture, forestry and fishing	11.2
Gross domestic product per head (1988, US $)	2 476	Mining and manufacturing	42.9
Gross fixed capital formation:		Building	6.2
1988 (billion dinars)	27 193	Other	39.7
1988 (per cent of GNP)	17.6		

GOVERNMENT

Government consumption (1988, per cent of GDP)	14.2	General government revenue, including social security	
		(1988, per cent of GDP)	32.0

FOREIGN TRADE

	Structure of exports in 1988 (per cent)	Structure of imports in 1988 (per cent)
Food, drinks, tobacco	8.3	6.0
Raw materials and semi-finished goods	34.0	26.5
Finished manufactures	46.2	31.8

THE CURRENCY

Monetary unit: Dinar	Currency units per US $, average of daily figures:	
Note: A new dinar equal to 10 000 old dinars was introduced on	Year 1988	2.714.6
18th December 1989.	Year 1989	33 060.58
	May 1990	11.7621

Note: An international comparison of certain basic statistics is given in an annex table.

Introduction

When Yugoslavia was last examined by the Economic and Development Review Committee in the Spring of 1988, the authorities were just about to introduce wide-ranging liberalisation measures in the field of prices, foreign-exchange allocation and imports as part of a reform process towards the establishment of a more market-oriented economy. With growing recognition that previous piecemeal reforms and stop-and-go measures had done more harm than good to the economy, the reform process gathered considerable momentum notably in 1989, enhancing the exposure of banks and socialised enterprises to market mechanisms and instruments of demand management. Most important measures were adopted in late 1989, and certain reforms are still being debated or await legislative acts before they can be implemented.

Against the background of this much-commended and applauded course of events the actual performance of the economy over the past two years has remained disappointing. While most OECD countries enjoyed high rates of economic growth, the level of output stagnated in Yugoslavia and despite weak domestic demand and rising unemployment the battle against inflation was lost. Indeed after the end of the partial price and wage freeze in May 1988 a powerful price-wage spiral was set in motion pushing the monthly rate of inflation to some 50 per cent by the end of 1989. The 1988-89 improvement of the balance-of-payments situation, the only visible bright spot in the otherwise bleak picture, owed more to the rapid expansion of world exports and sluggish home demand than to a strengthening of underlying trends.

To stop the runaway inflation within the shortest conceivable spell of time, the Government launched a tough and at the same time ingenious stabilisation programme, combining a Deutschemark-pegged new convertible dinar with a wage and partial price freeze and a tight macroeconomic policy stance. The aim is to bring the year-on-year rate of inflation down to 13 per cent by the end of 1990, accepting in the meantime a decline in output and real demand as well as a weakening in the current external balance from a comfortably-strong starting level. Before discussing the anti-inflation package in more detail and analysing its first encouraging results in Part III, the present Survey reviews in Part I the developments which have led to the spectacular acceleration of inflation during the last couple of years. The more deep-seated problems behind Yugoslavia's long-standing inflation proneness are recalled in Part II which also provides a critical assessment of the structural reform process. The main findings of the Survey and most important policy considerations are presented in the concluding chapter.

I. Developments in 1988 and 1989

Official targets and policy intentions

Since the mid-1980s the failure of earlier stabilisation efforts to break the vicious circle of stagflation[1] has been increasingly seen as a demonstration that restoration of a satisfactory and sustainable growth path was not possible without pervasive economic reforms involving far-reaching reconsiderations of basic policy approaches and fundamental principles of economic management. With economic results persistently and increasingly diverging from the annual targets of Economic Resolutions, the efficacy of administrative measures in controlling macroeconomic variables was more and more put into question. Indeed, the partial price freeze imposed in November 1987 after the year-on-year rate of consumer price inflation had reached 250 per cent was not particularly well adhered to and the risk of a renewed acceleration of the price/wage spiral was felt to be high in the spring of 1988. Faced with the prospect of intensified external and internal imbalances, the authorities, supported by an IMF stand-by arrangement and favourable agreements with commercial banks and official creditors on external financing, announced further restrictive fiscal, monetary and incomes policy measures in May 1988. At the same time the Government agreed on a comprehensive programme of price, import and foreign-exchange liberalisation[2]. This package of market-oriented measures was expected to contain inflation through positive demand and supply-side effects, to be reinforced by envisaged major reforms, notably in the field of the enterprise and the banking sector. However, as discussed further below, both the 1988 and the 1989 outcome betrayed the optimistic expectations reflected in the Economic Resolution targets.

Incomes and price policies

Concerned by the higher-than-targeted wage increases during the first five months of the year, in May 1988 the government fixed the permissible increase in wages at 122 per cent for 1988, slightly below the projected price increase, and announced stricter controls on wages by the Social Accounting Service (SDK)[3]. In 1989, in line with the new policy orientation of decontrolling markets, wage ceilings were lifted and wages allowed to be determined by market forces. However, in order to prevent an excessive wage growth at the expense of enterprises' profits the statutory minimum rate of accumulation (retained earnings) was raised from 3.5 per cent of fixed and working capital to nearly 4 per cent. Nonetheless strong wage cost pressure developed in the course of 1989. In order to stem runaway inflation and rapidly-rising enterprise losses the authorities reimposed wage restrictions in October 1989. It was decided to reduce retroactively monthly wage increases pertaining to August and September to 90 per cent of the increase in the cost of living. Further real wage restrictions were announced in the December anti-inflationary package (see Part III).

Parallel to the envisaged reduction of the aggregate rate of inflation to 95 per cent during 1988 and 60 per cent in 1989, another principal goal was the elimination of price "disparities" resulting from delayed adjustments in controlled prices and restrictions of foreign competition. Price liberalisation, while serving to correct distortions in the price structure, was expected to strengthen disinflation forces. By November 1988 some 70 per cent of industrial producer prices (somewhat less for consumer prices) had been fully liberalised, i.e. twice as many as a year earlier (see Part II). Moreover, the regime of administered prices (mainly public-utility prices) was phased out by May 1989 and the number of product prices requiring the approval by the Federal Bureau of Prices was reduced drastically. At the end of 1989 all indirect regimes of price control were abolished and the share of freely-determined prices was raised to 75 per cent. On the other hand, most product prices that had been previously subject to official approval have been temporarily brought back under the direct control of the Federal Government.

Monetary and fiscal targets

The announcement of restrictive monetary targets has been a key element of the anti-inflationary programmes of the past two years. In May 1988 the growth targets for the extension of net dinar credit by commercial banks and the National Bank of Yugoslavia (NBY) during 1988 were set at 26 per cent and 15 per cent respectively, implying in the absence of "valuation" effects[4] a marked deceleration in M2 growth during the second half of the year. It was also decided to raise the NBY's discount rate to a real positive level of 5 per cent, and banks' obligatory reserve requirements (at strongly negative real interest rates) were considerably increased during the year, but abolished for credits at the end of 1988. Moreover, the May 1988 package introduced price indexation of loans of one year or more and of deposits of three months or more. This meant a revaluation of the principal in line with the monthly retail price index. The minimum (real) interest rate on the indexed principal was fixed at 5 per cent for short-term deposits and at higher rates for longer-term deposits.

Seen against the rapid ratcheting-up of inflation the target growth for net dinar credits in 1989, set at 32.4 per cent, was also restrictive, perhaps even too restrictive to be credible. Further increases in obligatory reserve requirements on deposits were decided, bringing the ratio for most short-term deposits to 23 per cent, up from around 15 per cent two years earlier. The authorities reiterated their commitment to a positive real interest-rate policy but abrogated the obligation of banks to inflation-index deposits of less than one year. As far as exchange-rate policies are concerned, the authorities, following the introduction of a unified foreign-exchange market and the implementation of import liberalisation measures in the second half of 1988, declared that demand and supply would be the main determinants, with the NBY ready to intervene only in the event of excessive fluctuations.

Consolidation of public-sector finances, including a gradual reduction in the ratio of public expenditure to gross social product (GSP), has been a key objective since 1987. In 1988, except for pensions, most non-federal public expenditure categories were planned to increase by 10 percentage points less than GSP, to be achieved mainly via cuts in real wages and expenditure on goods and services. The 1989 Budget proposals were for a further, if small, reduction in the ratio of public-sector expenditure to 31 per cent of GSP but also for less generous pension rights, including stricter controls on invalidity pensions. In order to contain spending, a law was passed obliging social agencies ("self-managed communities of interest" for education, health, pensions and social welfare in general) with surpluses of more than 3 per cent of revenues in any given accounting period (usually three months) to reduce taxes and contributions. The law also stipulated that in case of higher-than-budgeted inflation, revenues should rise by 10 per cent less than the inflation overrun for government proper and 5 per cent less for social agencies.

Financial instability and slow growth

Hyperinflation

The release of pent-up pressures after the ending of the partial price freeze in June 1988 and the simultaneous liberalisation of price-fixing procedures, coupled

Diagram 1. **THE WAGE-PRICE SPIRAL**

Change over previous month[1]

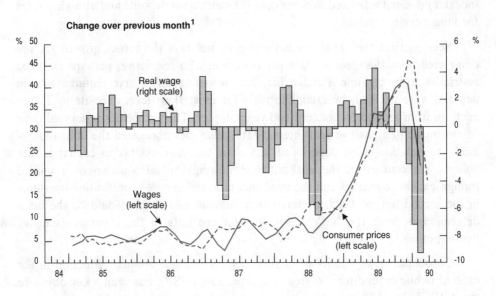

Year to year change

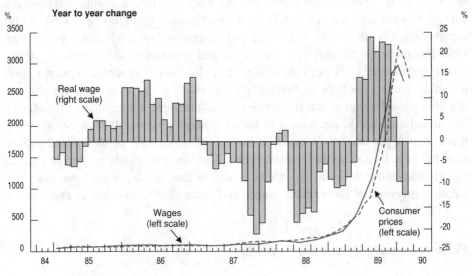

1. Data in the diagram show in which month payments are made and not the month to which payments actually pertain, as it is the case in Yugoslav statistics.

Source : Direct submission by Yugoslav authorities.

with a 25 per cent devaluation of the dinar, set in motion a powerful price-price spiral. Up to September the accompanying sharp decline in real labour costs had a damping impact on inflation, but in the face of mounting social tensions the authorities relaxed income norms in October 1988, immediately entailing across-the-board moves of recuperation of real income losses. Nominal wages rose by 15 per cent per month during the last quarter of 1988, about double the rate of the previous six months (Diagram 1).

The decision in 1989 to allow wages to be freely determined added further momentum to the inflation process both through wage-price and price-price spiralling effects, thus setting the stage for hyperinflation. The increase in real wages by some 20 per cent in the eight months to September 1989 was an important cost-push factor[5]. Irregular adjustments in controlled prices contributed to a continuous ratcheting-up of price increases and inflation expectations. A self-feeding process of runaway inflation developed in which producers selling on credit charged prices

Table 1. **Prices and wages**

Percentage change from previous year

	1986	1987	1988	1989	Dec. 86 / Dec. 85	Dec. 87 / Dec. 86	Dec. 88 / Dec. 87	Dec. 89 / Dec. 88
				Prices				
Producer prices								
Industrial goods	71	99	203	1 306	68	159	274	2 648
of which:								
Electricity	89	158	164	1 331	147	212	137	3 234
Agricultural goods	84	103	204	1 120	74	127	248	1 931
Retail prices	**88**	**118**	**199**	**1 256**	**92**	**168**	**251**	**2 665**
of which:								
Agricultural products	84	117	190	928	82	167	229	1 990
Industrial products	89	117	199	1 261	94	165	251	2 622
Consumer prices[1]	**89**	**120**	**195**	**1 252**	**91**	**171**	**241**	**2 714**
Goods	88	118	195	1 262	90	168	241	2 692
of which:								
Food	90	111	202	1 255	82	160	266	2 513
Services	95	138	194	1 188	97	180	240	2 872
				Wages				
Real wages, net[2,3]								
Socialised sector, total	9.3	4.1	−5.8	−0.4	13.3	−20.9	−5.0	5.8

1. Cost-of-living index.
2. The OECD has adjusted Yugoslav statistics so that the figures better reflect the period during which wages are actually paid and not the period during which wages pertain, as in the official Yugoslav statistics.
3. Between 1980 and 1985 the annual rate of change of consumers' prices was 47 per cent and of real wages in the socialised sector −4.5 per cent.

Sources: Indeks, Federal Statistical Office and data submitted by national authorities and OECD estimates.

15

significantly above current costs in anticipation of expected losses arising from the erosion of real money value by the time of actual payment. The annualised rate of increase in consumer prices reached 13 000 per cent during the fourth quarter of 1989 up from 500 per cent during the first quarter. Under these conditions it became increasingly evident that the dinar had lost two important functions: its utility as a store of value and as a unit of account. In the event the dinar was increasingly replaced by the Deutschemark in transactions of enterprises and households alike.

Describing the mechanics of inflation does not throw adequate light on its underlying causes. As discussed in Part II, the roots of Yugoslavia's inflation proneness have to be found in the lack of efficient market mechanisms and inadequate macroeconomic management. Despite measures taken to strengthen financial discipline of enterprises, it continued to be possible for enterprises to borrow on short term in order to finance excessive rises in wages and to calculate and to decide on the distribution of enterprise income on the basis of doubtful financial claims. Moreover, in a period of hyperinflation there are inevitable lags in adjusting asset values, making it relatively easy for self-managed enterprises to violate or circumvent existing statutory reserve and distribution ratios. Under these conditions, it was not surprising that the liberalisation of imports and a real appreciation of the dinar had no perceptible damping effect on inflation trends in 1989.

Domestic demand, net exports and production

The reported growth of real household income in 1988 owes much to the marked increase in interest receipts. However, to the extent that high nominal interest rates compensate for high and rising inflation, the real increase in interest receipts by households in 1988 was considerably less than shown in the statistics. Real household income, adjusted for financial wealth effects, broadly stagnated in 1988 as the inflation-induced erosion in the real value of dinar financial assets (the inflation tax) outweighed the positive wealth effect on households' foreign-exchange deposits resulting from the real depreciation of the dinar (the valuation effect). In 1989 the inflation tax combined with a negative valuation effect and falling emigrant remittances seem to have outweighed the increase in real wages. Yet, private consumption turned up and may have risen even more strongly than suggested by official data (Table 2). Part of the statistical discrepancy between output and demand measures of GSP seems indeed to reflect greater buoyancy of consumer spending, channelled through the black market and tax-free shops (in foreign currency). Consequently, a sharp drop in the saving rate from the high

16

Table 2. **Demand and output**[1]

	1988 Billion dinars current prices	1985 / 1980	1986	1987	1988	1989 official estimate
		Annual percentage change at constant prices				
Private consumption[2]	74.6	−0.8	4.5	0.3	−1.3	1.0
Public consumption[3]	13.0	−1.9	4.6	−1.5	0.1	−1.0
Fixed investment	27.2	−7.7	3.5	−5.1	−5.8	0.5
Final domestic demand	114.8	−3.0	4.2	−1.4	−2.2	0.6
Stockbuilding[4]	31.5	1.8	0.0	0.9	0.7	−1.9
Total domestic demand	**146.3**	**−1.0**	**3.4**	**−0.2**	**−1.1**	**−1.1**
Exports	46.6	0.0	2.0	−0.6	5.7	7.2
Imports	48.1	−7.2	8.8	−5.8	1.1	12.7
Foreign balance[4]	−1.4	1.5	−1.8	1.2	1.1	−1.1
Statistical discrepancy[4]	3.7	–	1.9	−2.1	−1.7	3.3
Gross social product	**148.6**	**0.8**	**3.6**	**−1.1**	**−1.7**	**0.8**
Agriculture and forestry	15.3	1.1	10.1	−4.0	−3.3	3.6
Other activities	133.3	0.7	2.5	−0.7	−1.4	0.4
Industry	71.0	2.7	3.9	0.8	−0.7	1.8
Construction	8.7	−6.6	−1.4	−0.9	−6.1	2.2
Services	53.6	0.2	1.7	−2.6	−1.3	−1.5

1. Yugoslav definitions and concepts.
2. Productive consumption only, i.e. excluding certain services amounting to 3.8 billion dinars in 1988.
3. "General and collective consumption" according to Yugoslav definitions, i.e., excluding government wages and salaries amounting to somewhat less than 10 billion dinars in 1988.
4. Percentage change contribution to the growth of the social product.
Sources: Statistical Yearbook of Yugoslavia, 1987, Saopstenje, Federal Statistical Office, and data submitted by the Federal Planning Office.

1987-1988 level seems to have taken place, reflecting consumers' preference for holding goods rather than cash in periods of accelerating inflation.

With shrinking real outlays on goods and services and on national defence, public-sector collective non-wage expenditure[6] fell in 1989 after broad stability in 1988. The decline in fixed investment, which had started in late 1986, came to a halt in 1989. As in 1988, "economic" investment in the private sector (i.e. excluding investment in housing) was buoyant, supported by the easing of restrictions on private initiative. In the socialised sector fixed net asset formation continued to fall, mainly reflecting a sharp drop in industrial investment in response to falling enterprise income, rising interest charges and uncertain demand prospects. By contrast, investment in transport, communications, trade and financial services held up much better. Investment in "non-economic" sectors remained weaker than in the socialised sector, notably in the area of public administration and in health and social

17

welfare. Similarly, residential investment continued to shrink, mainly due to reduced building activity by public agencies and socialised enterprises.

After two years of decline final domestic demand is reported to have increased in 1989 (Table 2) despite the likely under-recording of private consumption. Likewise, official statistics seem to exaggerate the negative contribution of stockbuilding[7], so that total domestic demand may also have grown in 1989, as is indeed suggested by import figures. The acceleration in the growth of export volumes was more than offset by brisk imports, following two years of sluggish import trends. This resulted in a negative contribution to GSP growth on a mechanical accounting basis. However, in a dynamic sense the marked increase in imports boosted production by relieving shortages of imported intermediate products, on which Yugoslav industry is heavily dependent.

Except for shrinking output in services, all other sectors shared the small growth of GSP in 1989. Within industry, light consumer goods recorded the biggest increase. However, more than one-half of the rise in GSP in 1989 is accounted for by higher agricultural output following two years of decline due to drought. Even so, agricultural output in 1989 was only some 10 per cent higher than in 1979: it grew at an annual rate of about one-third less than during the previous fifteen years. This disappointing performance stems from the restrictions on private farming, low guaranteed prices for certain products, inefficiencies in socialised farming and agro-food industries.

The labour market

The deceleration in the growth of GSP during the 1980s to less than 1 per cent per annum has been much more pronounced than that of employment growth. As a result, the average level of labour productivity actually fell by some 0.5 per cent per annum. Responding to political and social pressure, socialised enterprises continued to recruit labour irrespective of their real employment needs. Thus, up to 1987, employment growth in the socialised sector more than offset the contraction of the large private agricultural labour force. Industry contributed about one-half to the growth of employment in the socialised sector but experienced a loss of average productivity by nearly 4 per cent between 1979 and 1987 compared with an increase of one-fourth in OECD Europe.

With output continuing to fall, the relaxation of requirements for enterprises to increase employment each year together with other reform measures to reverse the downward path of productivity brought the previous strong rise of employment

Table 3. **Employment**

	1988 thousand	$\frac{1985}{1981}$	1986	1987	1988	1989
			Percentage change from previous year			
Population of working age	15 320	0.9	0.6	0.6	0.6	0.6
Domestic labour force[1]	10 085	1.5	1.5	1.5	1.4	1.3
Domestic employment	**9 539**	**1.2**	**1.8**	**2.1**	**-1.2**	**-0.3**
Private sector	2 824	-0.8	-0.7	-1.1	-1.3	-0.4
Agriculture	2 165	-2.5	-2.6	-2.7	-2.8	-2.9
Excl. agriculture	659	8.2	7.7	5.5	4.1	7.7
Self–employed	490	10.0	7.3	4.4	4.3	8.2
Paid employees	169	3.6	8.7	8.7	3.7	6.5
Socialised sector	**6 715**	**2.2**	**3.0**	**2.0**	**0.2**	**-0.2**
Agriculture	311	3.1	3.1	1.8	-0.7	-0.3
Excl. agriculture	6 404	2.2	2.9	2.1	0.2	-0.2
of which:						
Industry and mining	2 716	3.1	3.8	3.1	0.4	-0.1
Agriculture	**2 476**	**-1.9**	**-2.0**	**-2.2**	**-2.5**	**-2.5**
Non–agricultural sectors	**7 063**	**2.6**	**3.3**	**3.7**	**-0.7**	**0.5**
Memorandum items, thousand						
Job seekers[2]	1 132	920	1 087	1 081	1 132	1 190
(Per cent of domestic labour force)	(11.2)	(9.6)	(11.1)	(10.9)	(11.2)	(11.6)
Workers temporarily working abroad, thousands		768	770	775		

1. Economically active population minus workers temporarily employed abroad.
2. Including those at work but looking for another job (see text).
Sources: Indeks, Federal Statistical Office and data submitted by the Federal Planning office.

in the socialised sector to an end in early 1988. As the agricultural labour force continued to shrink, overall employment showed a small decline in 1988 for the first time since 1967. Despite some recovery of output total employment declined again in 1989, permitting some pick-up in overall labour productivity, the first since the end of the 1970s. In industry, productivity increased by 2 per cent in 1989 with most branches sharing the upturn (Table 3).

Private sector non-agricultural employment has been on a steep upward trend during the last fifteen years, especially during the 1980s when its annual rate of growth was nearly four times that of the socialised sector. However, given its still small size – 7 per cent of the active labour force – the impact on total employment has been rather modest. Most private-sector employment is in services, especially small shops, restaurants and other entertainment activities. It is also worth noting

Diagram 2. UNEMPLOYMENT RATE BY REGION

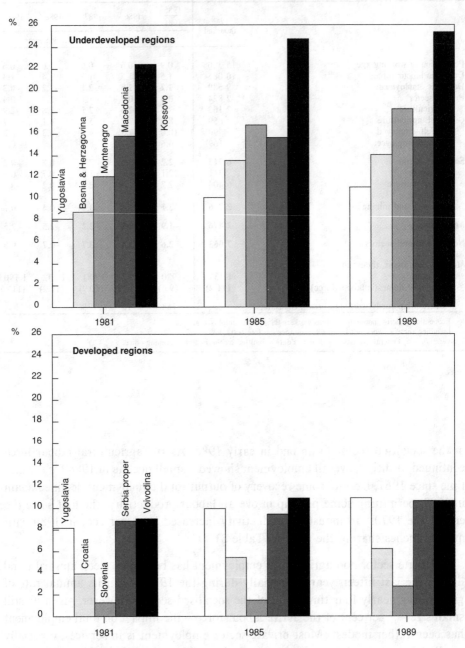

Source : Direct submission by Yugoslav authorities.

that the private share in non-agricultural employment in the most developed republics, Slovenia and Croatia, is not significantly higher than in the other republics and provinces.

The number of registered job-seekers, after a temporary decline in 1987, has since exhibited renewed buoyancy, reaching 1.2 millions in 1989 (11 per cent of the domestic labour force). The return of Yugoslav workers from abroad, which set in after the first oil shock, has continued through the 1980s at a fairly steady rate. More recently increased rationalisations and liquidations of enterprises have added to the pool of job-seekers. However, its recorded level overstates the actual number of jobless as it includes people already at work but looking for another job, and students looking for part-time or permanent jobs after the termination of their studies. Registered unemployment has increased only modestly since 1986, especially in 1989, pointing to a growing number of discouraged workers and probably more importantly, to a rising weight of the underground economy. In 1989, women accounted for slightly more than one-half of all registered job-seekers and, as in previous years, almost two-thirds, mostly youngsters under 25 years old, were new entrants into the labour force. There are large differences in regional unemployment rates[8] and the share of skilled jobless people is relatively high, pointing to important mismatches between labour demand and supply both on a geographical and on a professional basis (Diagram 2).

Foreign trade and payments

The policy-induced reduction in merchandise exports on a clearing basis since the mid-1980s[9] has depressed the overall growth of exports, reflecting the difficulties in switching production designed for COMECON and less-developed countries to OECD markets with high-quality standards. By 1989, the share of exports on a clearing basis has dropped to 20 per cent of total exports, i.e. to one-half that of 1985. Meanwhile, exports in convertible currencies continued to grow, though only in line with the growth of export markets. This performance underlines the importance of structural impediments, which offset the export-push stemming from the sluggishness in domestic demand and the significant real effective depreciation of the dinar between the end of 1987 and mid-1989.

Merchandise imports on a clearing basis further declined in 1989 mainly due to the smaller oil bill (Table 4). Nonetheless, total imports increased by some 12 to 13 per cent in value and probably over 10 per cent in volume (Diagram 3). Following broad stagnation in the first half of 1988 convertible-currency imports picked up sharply in response to the import-liberalisation process initiated in

Table 4. **Foreign trade**

Percentage change from previous year

	Exports f.o.b.					Imports f.o.b.				
	1985	1986	1987	1988	1989	1985	1986	1987	1988	1989
Total value (U.S. dollars)	4.3	4.3	6.0	8.3	6.1	2.4	7.1	-0.8	2.5	12.6
Price	-3.1	7.1	6.0	3.2	1.2	-0.1	0.5	6.7	3.3	-0.5
Volume	7.6	-2.6	0.0	4.9	4.8	2.5	6.6	-7.0	-0.9	13.2
Non-convertible currencies	12.5	-7.1	-15.9	-2.4	-3.6	-6.7	-15.1	1.3	-8.3	-2.8
Price	-1.0	0.0	1.3	2.5	4.4	1.9	-15.8	-2.6	2.3	2.9
Volume	13.6	-7.1	-17.0	-4.8	-7.7	-8.4	0.8	4.0	-10.4	-5.5
Convertible currencies	0.4	11.6	17.5	12.3	9.3	7.5	17.7	-1.5	6.3	17.2
Price	-4.2	11.4	7.9	3.4	0.3	-1.0	7.6	10.3	3.8	-1.3
Volume	4.0	0.2	8.9	8.6	9.0	8.6	9.4	-10.7	2.4	18.8
of which:										
OECD	2.1	20.7	27.8	16.5	7.1					
Price	-5.1	18.3	11.1	4.1	-1.0					
Volume	7.6	2.1	15.1	11.9	8.2					
Excluding oil:						6.6	21.9	0.6	4.8	17.3
Price						-1.0	15.1	9.2	3.9	-2.6
Volume						7.7	5.9	-7.9	0.9	20.4

Source: Federal Secretariat of Foreign Trade.

June 1988, growing in volume terms over 20 per cent, annual rate, in the second half of 1989. Particularly rapid was the growth of imports of consumer goods (almost 40 per cent in volume) in 1989 as a whole. These imports had earlier been suppressed through various barriers (see Part II) and liberalisation allowed the gradual release of pent-up demand for high-quality consumer goods.

The increase in the trade deficit in convertible currencies in 1989 was largely offset by a further steep rise in the invisible surplus. This favourable outcome owes much to the decline in the external debt and the related contraction of net interest payments. High inflation, financial instability and the associated low confidence explain the stagnation of reported net emigrant remittances in 1989 at their relatively low 1988 level[10]. However, there seems to have been some under-recording of remittances in 1989: an increasing proportion was probably kept in cash and many people paid directly in foreign exchange to buy tax-free goods in special shops following the extension of this privilege to residents at the end of 1988. As in 1988, uncertainty stemming from high inflation and erratic interest and exchange-rate changes has influenced the time profile of emigrant remittances: in the early months of 1989 there was a net outflow, prompting the authorities to raise interest rates on deposits held in DMs, Austrian schillings and Swiss francs and to suspend

Diagram 3. **FOREIGN TRADE PATTERNS**

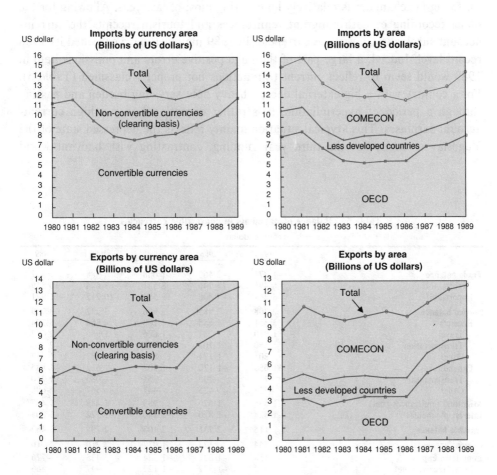

Source : Direct submission by Yugoslav authorities.

the restrictions on the amount that households could withdraw in cash from their foreign-exchange accounts. In the second quarter net emigrant remittances rebounded, with little further change in the remainder of the year.

Recorded foreign-exchange earnings from tourism in 1989 were broadly stable at just over $2 billion. However, actual receipts were apparently much higher as part of the earnings were channelled through the black market where the premium for foreign exchange was relatively high during most of last year. Allowing for the under-recording of both emigrant remittances and tourism receipts the current-account surplus in convertible currencies in 1989 may well have exceeded its 1988 record level. Indeed, a large part of the huge positive errors and omissions item in 1989 would seem to reflect current transactions not properly classified (Table 5). For a country with a big external debt, a heavy debt-servicing burden and passing through a period of hyperinflation, it is rather exceptional to run high current-account surpluses. This atypical situation mainly reflects the depressed state of the Yugoslav economy for the third year running, contrasting with buoyant world

Table 5. **Balance of payments in convertible currencies**

Million dollars

	1985	1986	1987	1988	1989
Trade balance	−1 771	−2 562	−1 068	−588	−1 452
Exports, fob	6 496	7 246	8 521	9 624	10 519
Imports, cif	−8 267	−9 808	−9 589	−10 212	−11 971
Service balance	2 308	2 985	2 906	3 232	3 769
Receipts	3 361	4 155	4 208	4 884	5 704
Travel	1 010	1 282	1 606	1 966	2 047
Transportation	1 550	1 702	1 730	2 035	2 100
Other	801	1 171	872	883	1 557
Expenditure	−1 053	−1 170	−1 302	−1 652	−1 935
Transportation	−715	−745	−855	−1 085	−1 250
Other	−338	−425	−447	−567	−685
Migrants' remittances (net)	1 635	1 620	989	1 488	1 497
Interest payments	−1 828	−1 870	−1 790	−1 922	−1 804
Invisible balance	2 115	2 735	2 105	2 798	3 462
Current account	344	173	1 037	2 210	2 010
Long-term capital	−158	−1 622	−1 324	−433	−776
Loans received, net	−63	−1 392	−1 122	−447	−566
Drawings[1]	3 183	2 792	2 837	1 627	1 145
Repayments	−3 246	−4 184	−3 959	−2 074	−1 711
Loans extended, net	−95	−230	−202	−75	−125
Short-term capital	−96	−36	350	−267	−237
Errors and omissions	58	1 565	−722	−72	1 661
Change in external reserves (− = decrease)	208	466	−1 074	1 549	2 835
Memorandum items:					
Refinancings	–	1 650	1 747	200	150
Official reserves	2 959	3 326	2 565	4 191	6 040
of which:					
Excluding gold	1 095	1 460	698	2 298	4 136
Current account balance in per cent of GSP	0.1	0.0	2.2	5.4	4.9

1. Including refinancing.
Source: National Bank of Yugoslavia.

demand; but to some extent it can also be explained by the persistence of trade barriers for a number of goods notwithstanding recent liberalisation measures.

The substantial current-account surpluses of the last few years permitted Yugoslavia to build up foreign-exchange reserves of more than $6 billion by the end of 1989 from the depleted level of $0.7 billion at the end of 1987. Net external indebtedness was further reduced in 1989 by buying back some $1.4 billion medium- to long-term loans from commercial banks at a considerable discount[11]. As a result, the external debt in convertible currencies declined from its peak level of $20 billion in 1987 to $16.2 billion at the end of 1989, with interest payments falling from 10.4 per cent to 7.8 per cent of current account receipts in convertible currencies.

The economic policy response

Monetary and exchange-rate developments

Contrary to policy intentions, the monetary stance continued to be accommo-dating in both 1988 and 1989. The official M2 target, which excludes valuation effects, was exceeded by a factor of six in 1988 and a factor of seventeen in 1989. Overall liquidity was boosted not only by an overproportionate increase in foreign-exchange deposits but also by the devaluation of the dinar, which automatically translates into higher foreign-exchange deposits at current dinar value. The valua-tion effect accounted for nearly two-thirds of the expansion of M2 in both years (Diagram 4). As a result, the share of foreign-exchange deposits in all deposits rose from 44 per cent at the end of 1986 to 62 per cent at the end of 1988 and further to almost 70 per cent by the end of 1989. For households the share exceeded 75 per cent at the end of 1989 up from 63 per cent in 1986.

In 1988, the upward trend in money velocity was interrupted as the indexation of the principal together with positive real interest rates led to a strong increase in dinar time deposits. Similarly, the real depreciation of the dinar and rising interest rates boosted foreign-exchange deposits. In 1989, the upward trend in money velocity resumed, with M2 in real terms declining by 20 per cent. A number of factors contributed to this decline. Firstly, negative real interest rates on dinar deposits since mid-1989 and rapidly-rising inflation expectations caused a flight out of the dinar. Secondly, foreign-exchange deposits shrank, *inter alia*, reflecting reduced emigrant remittances and a rush to buy goods in duty-free shops. Political

Table 6. Selected monetary aggregates

Percentage change from previous year

	Outstanding at the end of 1988 billions of dinars	1986	1987	1988			1989			
				II	III	IV	I	II	III	IV
Currency in circulation	5 852	111	85	122	128	172	196	368	777	2 015
Dinar sight deposits	19 342	108	106	140	192	243	246	394	724	1 908
Dinar saving and time deposits	16 975	87	58	100	141	184	318	457	732	2 378
Foreign exchange deposits	58 855	68	204	247	275	276	433	591	1 027	2 477
Money supply (M2)	101 024	85	130	179	217	243	356	518	906	2 325
(Real M2)		(-3.6)	(-13.9)	(7.7)	(-0.0)	(-2.3)	(-7.9)	(-17.5)	(-21.6)	(-11.0)
Net foreign liabilities	49 702	64	179	213	206	219	358	403	640	1 128
Domestic credit	95 962	85	108	147	189	240	365	508	884	2 498
Other net domestic assets[1]	54 764	60	250	271	263	226	341	422	699	934
Inter-enterprise credit	77 964	70	126	183	223	238				

1. This item essentially reflects valuation effects.
Source: Direct submission by the Yugoslav authorities.

Diagram 4. **SOURCES OF MONEY SUPPLY GROWTH**

Variations from same period of previous year, in per cent

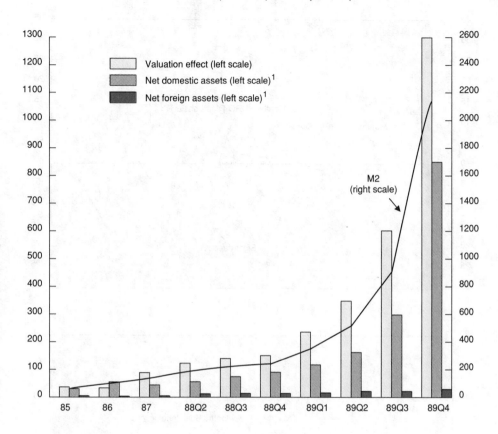

1. Excluding valuation effects.

Source : National Bank of Yugoslavia. *Quarterly Bulletin.*

and social tensions may also have induced households to hoard foreign-exchange receipts in cash instead of depositing them with banks.

The main sources of prime money supply in recent years have been the growing current-account surpluses in non-convertible currencies and higher-than-projected balance-of-payments surpluses in convertible currencies. But more

Diagram 5. **REAL INTEREST RATES** [1]

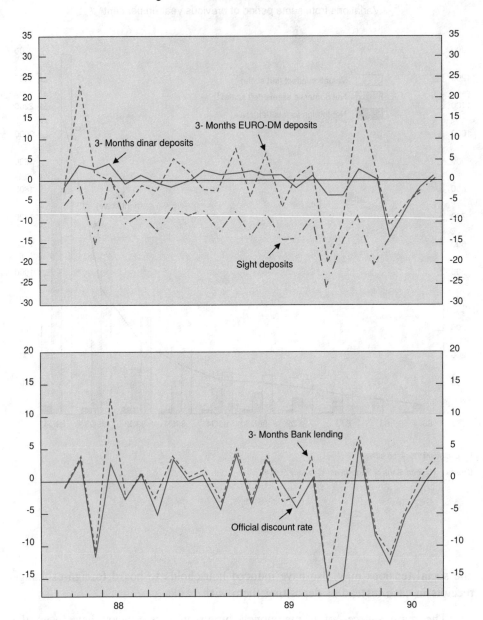

1. Nominal monthly interest rates deflated by monthly inflation rate.

Source :   National Bank of Yugoslavia. *Quarterly Bulletin.*

importantly for explaining the overshooting of the broader monetary targets has been the lack of NBY control over the supply of selective credits and the long tradition of banks of satisfying clients' credit demand with little regard to the NBY's directives (see Part II). Moreover, as noted above, banks have not yet stopped the practice of extending credits to enterprises which have run into cash-flow problems because of their "benign" neglect of doubtful financial assets. Further evidence of the persistent lack of discipline in the banking sector is the decline of banks' obligatory reserve ratio in 1989 contrary to the original goal of raising it by 2 percentage points. The discontinuation of the positive real interest-rate policy after mid-1989 contributed to the easing of monetary conditions and could be interpreted as a relaxation of the anti-inflationary policy stance in the course of 1989 (Diagram 5). Admittedly, the pursuit of a positive real-interest-rate policy in a period of rapidly and erratically-accelerating inflation poses important technical difficulties of monetary management. The frequent monthly swings from positive to negative real interest rates and *vice versa* in the last couple of years[12] bear witness to the formidable problems of controlling monetary flows in a period of hyperinflation.

Like interest rates, the real effective exchange rate has followed an erratic pattern since the end of 1987, with particularly large monthly variations occurring in the second half of 1989 (Diagram 6). Technical difficulties in forecasting monthly increases in prices and wages, in assessing the underlying inflation trend and the competitive effects of changes in cross exchange rates explain much of the apparent volatility of real exchange rates. However, the authorities appear also to have sought to pursue conflicting objectives with the same instrument. The exchange rate was used alternately for improving external competitiveness and for combating inflation. The latter goal seems to have carried more weight in the second half of the year when in the face of large current-account surpluses the dinar was permitted to appreciate markedly in real terms. In November the excessive rise of the preceding two months of nearly 30 per cent in real terms was partly corrected, bringing the real appreciation of the dinar down to 13 per cent during 1989 and keeping the real effective rate considerably below its average level of the 1980s.

Budgetary developments

Accelerating inflation and large swings in real wages have greatly affected budget developments in recent years. In 1988, the real wage fall of some 6 per cent in the public sector entailed an only slightly smaller reduction in inflation-adjusted

Diagram 6. **EXCHANGE-RATE DEVELOPMENTS**[1]

December 1982 = 100

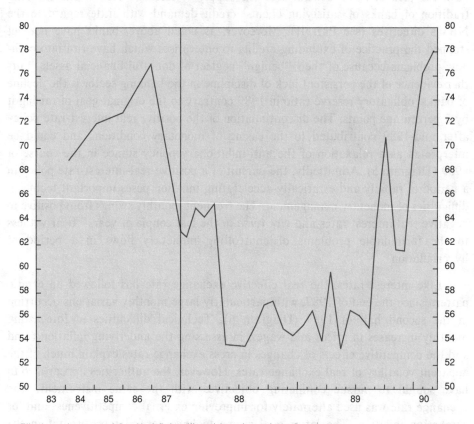

1. Effective exchange rate deflated by inflation differentials against major trading partners.

Source :   National Bank of Yugoslavia.

current expenditure on goods and service and social-security payments, thus helping to bring further down the ratio of public expenditure to GSP (to 31.3 per cent). In particular, real pension outlays fell by 11 per cent, largely reflecting delays in adjusting pensions in times of accelerating inflation. Direct taxes also fell somewhat in real terms in line with the fall in wages. By contrast, there was a substantial real increase in the turnover tax (in part due to a shift from specific to *ad valorem* taxes on oil and derivatives) and custom duties (by nearly one-fifth), reflecting the surge of imports of highly-taxed consumer goods. The consolidated public-sector accounts on a cash basis showed a small surplus in 1988. However, allowing for increased payment delays and, more importantly, the sizeable increase of the NBY's foreign-exchange liabilities in dinar terms (the valuation effect) the public-sector accounts were again in deficit to the tune of around 5 per cent of GSP.

Table 7. **Consolidated public sector accounts**[1]

	Billion dinars		Per cent of GSP			
	1988	1989	1986	1987	1988	1989
Revenue						
Direct taxes[2]	29 118	479 038	22.9	21.7	19.6	24.1
Indirect taxes	15 212	156 971	9.7	8.9	10.2	7.9
Other taxes and non-tax revenues	2 661	31 829	2.1	1.9	1.8	1.6
Total revenue	46 966	667 838	34.7	32.6	31.6	33.7
Expenditure						
National defence and administration	10 380		8.2	7.6	7.0	
Education	6 116		4.7	4.4	4.1	
Social security and welfare	20 058		14.6	15.4	13.5	
Intervention in the economy	5 004		3.5	3.1	3.4	
Other expenditure[3]	4 992		3.4	1.7	3.4	
Total expenditure	46 550		34.4	32.4	31.3	
Balance	416		0.3	0.2	0.3	

Note: Data may not add due to rounding.
1. Net of intra-public sector transfers; including communities of interest but excluding the Federal Fund for the Development of Underdeveloped Republics and Provinces.
2. Includes taxes on income and profits of enterprises and individuals, social security contributions, employers' payroll taxes and property taxes.
3. Includes housing expenditure, investment and current subsidies.
Source: Data submitted by national authorities.

In the first half of 1989, public revenues on an inflation-adjusted basis declined by one-fourth in real terms, giving rise to a large cash deficit, financed by resort to NBY loans. The lowering of certain social security contribution rates at the end of 1988 (applying to social agencies which had accumulated surpluses in previous accounting periods) and the abolition of import taxes on goods to be processed for exports led to a once-and-for-all fall in real revenues. But more importantly, there was an inflation-generated shortfall in the real value of turnover tax receipts, reflecting the delay between sales and enterprises' payments of the related turnover tax.

The government introduced corrective measures in mid-1989 to strengthen its financial position. The permissible delay for paying indirect taxes by enterprises was reduced in stages from twenty days to eight days by the end of the year. The turnover tax rate was raised by 2.6 percentage points to 20 per cent and some social security contribution rates were also put up. These measures combined with an increase in direct taxes led to an acceleration in net revenues and, by the end of 1989, the earlier revenue shortfall was broadly recuperated. In addition, the federal government started to reduce defence expenditure. The improvement in the accounts by the end of the year was such that, despite the incorporation of off-budget items in the federal budget in the second half of the year, the consolidated public-sector accounts on a cash basis were roughly in balance but public expenditure remained broadly stable as a per cent of GSP in 1989 as a whole. In all, even allowing for some lengthening of payment delays in government spending, the consolidated public-sector account on an accrual basis seems to have swung from a large deficit in 1988 to broad balance or perhaps even to a small surplus in 1989.

II. Market-oriented institutional and structural reforms

Yugoslavia has for long been in the vanguard of change among communist-ruled countries. The centralised planning of the economy, adopted after the second world war, was abandoned by the end of the 1950s though on the level of republics and provinces important elements of planning persisted until the mid-1970s. In the early 1950s, a unique economic system based on the principle of workers' self-management was introduced. Being credited for the rapidly rising per capita incomes during its first 20 years of existence and appreciated for its comparatively high degree of democracy in work-related matters, the "Yugoslav model" was studied with great interest both for its apparent merits and for its perhaps less-publicised drawbacks by many economic analysts and political observers alike.

However, during the past two decades clouds have been covering the hitherto seemingly bright horizon, putting at risk the prospect of progressively catching up with the living standards of more advanced industrialised countries. Indeed, the Yugoslav economy entered the 1980s with growing current balance-of-payments deficits which were only in part the result of external factors such as the two oil price hikes in 1973/74 and 1979 and the related temporary stagnation of export markets in industrial countries. Much more important were the excessively ambitious and unbalanced economic growth strategy pursued throughout the 1970s and the inadequate response of domestic supply and savings, implying heavy reliance on imports and foreign borrowing. In 1980 the external debt in convertible currencies had reached more than a quarter of GSP and rigidities on the supply side of the economy made it difficult to generate the surplus necessary to service this debt.

Since 1980 Yugoslavia has taken almost continuous commitments with the Bretton Woods institutions and its creditors to correct its external deficit and improve its economic structures. Five stand-by arrangements with the IMF, one structural adjustment loan with the World Bank and one enhanced surveillance procedure with the IMF, together with several rescheduling arrangements with

33

Table 8. **Medium-term performance**

	Yugoslavia[1]	Spain	Portugal	Turkey	OECD
	Annual percentage change				
1965-73					
Output growth	6.2	6.4	7.2	6.7	5.2
Inflation	11.7	6.9	3.6	11.5	4.9
Real GDP per head	5.2	5.3	7.4	4.1	4.2
Current account (per cent of GDP)	(–0.4)	(–0.4)	(2.4)	(0.0)	(0.3)
1974-80					
Output growth	6.4	2.1	3.3	4.0	2.6
Inflation	17.9	17.9	21.7	42.9	9.9
Real GDP per head	5.3	1.0	1.8	1.8	1.9
Current account (per cent of GDP)	(–3.1)	(–1.6)	(–3.7)	(–3.2)	(–0.2)
1981-89					
Output growth	0.6	2.8	2.4	4.8	2.9
Inflation	138.7	9.5	17.9	43.5	5.0
Real GDP per head	–0.2	2.0	1.5	2.7	2.1
Current account (per cent of GDP)	(1.6)	(–0.8)	(–3.0)	(–2.0)	(–0.4)
Memorandum items:					
Labour productivity (1988)[2]	16	73	25	12	100
Average monthly wages in US dollars (1988)	290	1 035	361	153	1697[3]
	1965	1973	1980	1987	March 1990
	Billion US dollars				
Gross foreign debt of Yugoslavia	1.3	4.7	18.9	22.0	18.1

1. For Yugoslavia, GDP refers to GSP.
2. OECD average equals 100. Labour productivity is measured as the ratio of GDP in dollars at current prices to total employment.
3. Average for the major seven OECD countries.
Sources: National Bank of Yugoslavia and OECD, *National Accounts*.

official creditors and commercial banks, attest to Yugoslavia's persistent efforts in the 1980s to tackle structural weaknesses and indicate the strong financial support received from abroad. While these efforts and accompanying measures in conjunction with the implementation of successive stabilisation programmes have succeeded in strengthening the external balance and in reducing foreign indebtedness, the overall performance of the Yugoslav economy during the 1980s has been very disappointing (Table 8). Incomes per head have stagnated in real terms, while at the same time prices have shown a marked tendency to accelerate in spite of recurrent recourse to price controls.

The systemic weaknesses of the Yugoslav economy lying behind the failure to return it to a higher and sustainable growth path have become increasingly evident during the 1980s and have been identified in previous *OECD Economic Surveys of Yugoslavia*, notably the lack of adequate incentives in goods and factor markets, and insufficient and ineffective monetary and fiscal policy instruments. These institutional and structural problems will be briefly recalled in the following section before providing an overview and assessment of basic reform measures in the remainder of this chapter.

Inflation proneness and misallocation of resources

Lack of market incentives and penalties

a) *High wage disbursement of enterprise income*

Socialised enterprises in Yugoslavia are based and run on two crucial principles: social ownership of means of production and workers' self-management. According to the 1974 Federal Constitution a socialised enterprise belongs to all Yugoslavs collectively but to nobody individually. The workers' council, acting on behalf of the workers, is responsible for the management of the enterprise including the appointment of acting managers though in practice there is also strong influence from local political forces. It follows from the above that workers, if left free to decide, could fully withdraw the income or cash-flow generated by the use of the socialised capital without giving due regard to who has to bear possible current or future losses arising from excessive wage increases or under-capitalisations. Hence, there is a strong built-in tendency in self-managed enterprises to maximise the workers' income share while limiting saving for reinvestment in the own enterprise and even more so for investment into other companies.

Various types of regulatory safeguards, notably the imposition of ceilings to wage increases and of minimum investment or compulsory accumulation ratios, have been used to limit the rise in labour incomes. In 1976, socially-owned enterprises were transformed into "organisations of associated labour" (OAL). Within each OAL "basic organisations of associated labour" (BOAL) were created which were endowed with considerable management autonomy. This move towards further decentralisation which was supposed to enhance the efficiency of the system by giving workers more responsibilities in decision-making and a greater say in the internal income distribution proved, however, to be counterproductive in that it added to bureaucracy and overhead costs as well as to frictions in the running of enterprises.

In spite of the safeguards to contain excessive pay increases, the saving rate (net of depreciation) of enterprises has sharply declined since the mid-1980s from an already low level (Diagram 7). In fact, at the end of the decade, the net saving rate was strongly negative, implying that revenues no longer covered current expenditures. Investment by enterprises has also declined dramatically, though less so than retained earnings, entailing a rise in borrowing requirements. Some of the borrowing needs could be met by recourse to a special fund, which is essentially financed by enterprises. However, the total amount deposited in this fund is small. It represented in 1988 less than 1 per cent of total borrowing requirements. Local authorities and the governments of republics and autonomous provinces have also helped in the past to cover enterprises' deficits and to finance investments. But recourse to bank credit is typically the main source of finance.

b) *Soft-budget constraint on enterprises*

In the absence of a capital market, banks are virtually the sole intermediary between lenders and borrowers of financial resources. However, the institutional subordination of banks to enterprises prevents an efficient allocation of national savings. Banks are founded and managed by enterprises (see below). The basic objective of banks has therefore always been to provide credits to founders at the lowest possible cost. This means little or no regard is paid to the profitability of banking operations. In principle, each bank founder has equal rights for the management of the bank, irrespective of the equity share. In reality, local authorities, who tend to favour big investment projects, exert a considerable influence over banks' decisions, with the result that big debtors have a particularly strong position in the management of banks.

As a consequence, socialised enterprises have operated under soft-budget constraints. Firms have been financially supported or subsidised in various ways, notably by cheap credits, usually with strongly negative real interest rates, and by resort to bank-guaranteed inter-enterprise credit with detrimental implications for the allocation of scarce national financial resources. Real lending rates have been particularly low for selective credits, provided by banks to so-called "priority" sectors, essentially agricultural and export activities, and rediscounted by the NBY. Until recently, interest rates on selective credits lay below the official discount rate (Table 9). *Ex post* the cost of borrowing has been further reduced by frequent write-offs of bank loans. The accommodating stance of the NBY has facilitated the cheap credit policy of banks, in particular the generous treatment of exchange-rate-induced increases of banks' dinar liabilities *vis-à-vis* households as liabilities of the NBY towards the banks[13]. The artificially-low cost of borrowing is

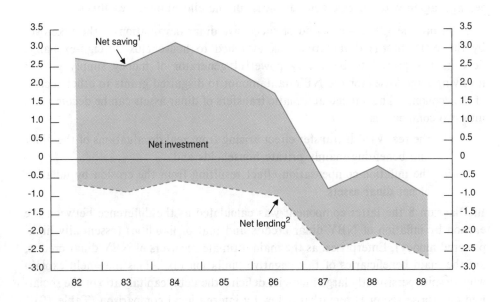

Diagram 7. **NET SAVING AND DEFICIT OF ENTERPRISES**

Per cent of enterprises revenues

1. Net of depreciation.
2. The minus sign indicates a borrowing position.

Source : Social accounting service.

Table 9. **Indicators for the soft–budget constraint**

	1980	1981	1982	1983	1984	1985	1986	1987	1988
Lending interest rates real[1]									
Commercial banks									
3-month loans:									
Minimum	−20.7	−19.7	−17.9	−18.8	−3.9	−8.8	−16.2	−14.5	−24.3[2]
Maximum	−18.5	−17.5	−8.8	−13.8	5.9	−0.2	−4.5	−6.3	9.6[2]
Selective credits	−24.7	−23.5	−19.7	−25.0	−9.8	−15.6	−16.1	−14.1	−20.2[2]
Write-off of loans									
(per cent of commercial bank loans)	0.0	0.0	0.0	0.1	0.2	0.2	0.2	3.5	3.1
Inter–enterprise credit									
(per cent of total bank credit)	38.8	38.6	37.5	42.4	43.9	47.4	44.5	42.0	44.8

1. Deflated by the twelve-month increase in the consumer price index.
2. Deflated by the annualised three-month increase in the consumer price index.
Source: National Bank of Yugoslavia, *Quarterly Bulletin;* and direct submission by the Yugoslav authorities.

probably the most important single factor behind the lack of industrial adjustment, as ailing firms have been kept afloat. In addition, the demand for credit has tended to exceed the supply for funds. This explains the frequent imposition of credit ceilings, again with adverse consequences for the allocation of resources.

During the 1980s – a period of successive dinar devaluations – the take-over by the NBY of the devaluation risk attached to households' foreign-exchange deposits has proved to be a very powerful generator of money supply growth involving huge losses for the NBY tantamount to disguised grants to other sectors of the economy. The implied automatic transfers of dinar assets can be decomposed into two components:

 i) the real-wealth-transfer effect arising from real devaluations of the dinar and benefiting mainly private households and

 ii) the inflation-compensation effect resulting from the erosion by inflation of net dinar assets.

In Diagram 8 the latter component was calculated as the difference between the erosion by inflation of NBY dinar credits and that of liabilities (essentially high-powered money). Enterprises, as the main ultimate receivers of NBY dinar credits, are the main beneficiaries of this negative "inflation tax". This may help explain why, despite persistently large financial deficits, the debt/capital ratio of the socialised enterprise sector is remarkably low by international comparison (Table 10).

Table 10. **Debt/equity ratios of non-financial enterprises**

	1972	1984
Yugoslavia	**1.1**	**1.2**
United States	1.7	1.5
Japan	..	3.8
Germany	1.8	1.6
France	..	2.4
Italy	2.3	2.1[1]
United Kingdom	..	1.2
Canada	0.8	0.7
Austria	1.4	1.6
Belgium	..	2.1
Denmark	..	1.3
Finland	..	4.3
Netherlands	..	1.3
Norway	..	5.2
Spain	..	1.7
Sweden	..	1.9

1. Refers to the year 1983.
Source: OECD, *Non-financial enterprises financial statements*, Paris, 1988.

Diagram 8. DISGUISED NBY TRANSFERS
Per cent of GSP

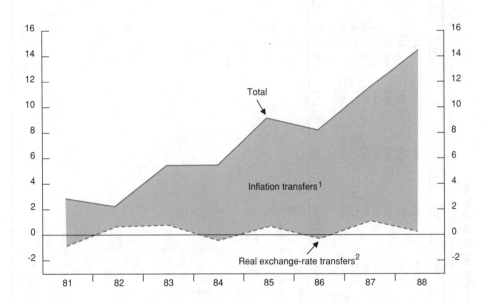

1. The inflation transfer is measured by the product of the inflation rate and NBY net dinar assets.
2. The real exchange-rate transfer is obtained as the rate of change of the real dinar/DM exchange rate times the net foreign exchange liabilities of the NBY.

Sources :   National Bank of Yugoslavia, *Quarterly Bulletin* and OECD estimates.

The gap between the effective cost of credit paid by borrowers and the cost that would have been charged if "normal" market conditions had prevailed, represents in reality an implicit subsidy to the non-financial sector (essentially enterprises). As shown in Table 11, the effective rate of return of the banking system has been increasingly negative, paralleling rising negative real costs of borrowing. In spite of the marked increase in the rate of return of commercial banks' operations since 1986, associated with the application of the 1987 accounting law (see below), the overall rate of return on banking operations has not stopped falling, due to rising NBY losses. Assuming a normal real cost of credit of 2 per cent, roughly equivalent to the growth potential of the Yugoslav economy, the implicit subsidy, i.e. the gap between the actual (negative) rate of return on the

39

Table 11. **Implicit bank subsidies to enterprises**

End of period, billion dinars

	1980	1981	1982	1983	1984	1985	1986	1987	1988
Commercial bank losses[1]	-23	-34	-98	-180	-350	-461	-265	1 442	2 291
NBY exchange-rate loss[2]	-76	-73	-226	-561	-907	-1 438	-2 707	-12 419	-45 693
Total bank losses	-99	-107	-324	-741	-1 257	-1 899	-2 972	-10 977	-43 402
Normal bank surplus[3]	52	72	101	148	231	389	641	1 551	5 547
Total bank subsidies[4]	151	179	425	889	1 488	2 288	3 613	12 528	48 949
(In per cent of bank assets)	(5.8)	(5.0)	(8.5)	(12.0)	(12.9)	(11.8)	(11.3)	(17.9)	(16.1)
(In per cent of GSP)	(8.0)	(7.0)	(12.2)	(17.1)	(16.9)	(13.7)	(10.1)	(12.9)	(15.1)
Memorandum item:									
Commercial banks' assets	2 615	3 598	5 026	7 402	11 534	19 433	32 044	77 547	277 333

1. Sum of the operating deficits, write-off of loans and net deferred foreign-exchange losses.
2. Increase in net foreign liabilities of NBY coming from dinar devaluations.
3. Assuming a "normal" intermediation margin of 2 per cent, the normal surplus is 2 per cent of bank assets.
4. Normal bank surplus minus total bank losses.
Source: Jugoslavensko Bankarstvo and OECD estimates.

assets of the banking system and the postulated or warranted real cost of credit of 2 per cent seems large by all standards.

Non-competitive market structures

a) Barriers to foreign competition

Inward-leaning economic developments and strategies have led over the years to inefficient import substitution at the expense of exports. They have also favoured the fragmentation of markets and restrictive business practices. Traditional protectionist instruments – customs duties, quotas, licences – have until recently been supplemented by strict rationing of scarce convertible current receipts from exports. A complex system of administratively determined, largely *ad hoc*, allocations of foreign exchange, based on individual enterprises', branches' and regions' import records and/or export receipts was established, thereby further strengthening oligopolistic market structures. The fact that a large part of trade has for long been on a clearing basis has provided little incentives to improve quality, thereby weakening competitive and innovative attitudes. Distorted price relationships of tradeables have given wrong signals to economic agents with adverse consequences for the expansion of potential growth and export activities.

b) Non-competitive domestic production structure

One fundamental weakness of the self-management system has been the low mobility of capital[14] which has been aggravated by the fact that economic development has been to a large extent planned and implemented by republican and provincial governments. The institutional set-up has encouraged vertical integration and oligopolistic behaviour in a context of regional autarky. The same industries were built in several republics and provinces, leading to over-capacity at the national level. Nationalistic tendencies have reinforced the segmentation of the Yugoslav market. This is underlined by the fact that trade between the eight republics and provinces declined considerably during the 1970s to around 22 per cent of all trade in 1980. Since then, the situation does not seem to have changed significantly, so that inter-republican trade has in relative terms remained below that, for example, among most EC countries.

The organisation of the banking sector has been an important factor behind the fragmentation of the Yugoslav market. The 165 basic banks and the even greater number of internal banks are mostly regional banks and competition among them is very limited. Internal banks are directly tied to a few enterprises. Basic banks are also established and controlled by the "founding" enterprises but have more extensive commercial activities. Given the dominant influence of borrowers, real banking and solvency criteria have typically ranked low in credit decisions. With relatively easy access to subsidised selective credits through the NBY and with interest rates on deposits often below current or expected rates of inflation, banks have been encouraged rather than discouraged to keep loss-making "owner-client" enterprises in operation.

The organisation and functioning of Yugoslav product markets are equally characterised by idiosyncrasies which negatively impinge on competition and economic efficiency. The distribution system is subordinate to industry. Wholesale and retail outlets are not supposed to maximise profits but just to cover costs and maintain adequate reserves. They are linked to specific (mainly local) producers with long-term agreements and often are simply part of vertically-integrated big industrial conglomerates. Located in the same republic or province they tend to be subject to local political pressure to give priority to local products. Independent trading enterprises, which could search for the cheapest suppliers, are relatively few.

The interest of local political forces to maintain control over economic activities – for ideological and/or more practical reasons – may help explain the various restrictions which, until recently, applied to private-sector initiative. Private companies could not employ more than 10 people, though in certain regions, with the connivance of the authorities, the limits were not always observed. Private farms were limited to 10 hectares (and up to 100 hectares in mountain areas) and access to credit was also restricted. Wholly-foreign-owned companies were practically non-existent. Though private companies have carved out a niche for themselves in the market and are usually doing well, their small size and the fact that very few of them are engaged in industrial activities made it impossible for them to challenge the large inefficient socialised enterprises and instil more competitive behaviour in the Yugoslav economy. Barriers to entry applied not only to private business but also to socialised companies if thus threatened the regional or local monopoly of large conglomerates.

Autarkic and protectionist attitudes of republics and local governments have favoured monopolistic and oligopolistic pricing policies in the socialised sector. Local monopolies in certain key areas, such as in bread production (e.g. one enterprise accounts for 80 per cent of bread production in Belgrade) have certainly reinforced the inflation-proneness of the economy. Enterprises unable to benefit from economies of scale often made cartel agreements, which were more or less openly endorsed by republican and provincial authorities[15]. The uneven incidence of

Diagram 9. **REGIONAL PRICE DISPARITIES**
Retail prices in 1988

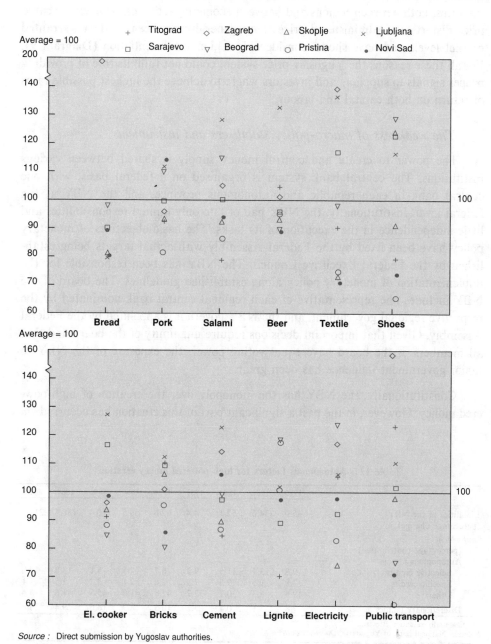

Source : Direct submission by Yugoslav authorities.

various direct and indirect subsidies (by local authorities, by the NBY for selective credits, by writing-off "bad" loans to enterprises, etc.) and differences in indirect tax rates, both between regions and between economic activities, have exacerbated price distortions. Administered prices have generally not been fixed at warranted market levels and have shown considerable regional differentiation (Diagram 9). For all these reasons the Yugoslav price system could not fulfil its role of providing proper signals to suppliers and investors where to achieve the highest possible rates of return on both capital and labour.

The weakness of macro-policy stabilisers and instruments

The power to create and control money supply is shared between various institutions. The central bank system is organised on a federal basis, with one central bank in each republic and autonomous province, and the NBY at the federal level. Institutionally, the NBY had of late only limited responsibilities and little independence in the execution of its tasks. The basic objectives of monetary policy have been fixed by the Federal Assembly with actual targets being established by the Federal Executive Council. The NBY has been responsible for the implementation of monetary policy along established guidelines. The board of the NBY includes one representative of each regional central bank nominated by the respective regional government, and the NBY governor is appointed by the Federal Assembly. Given that important decisions require unanimity of the board and that all members of the board have equal voting power, the exposure of the NBY to junior government influence has been great.

Constitutionally, the NBY has the monopoly over the creation of high-powered money. However, in the past a significant part of this creation has occurred *via*

Table 12. **Autonomous factors for high-powered money creation**

	1980	1981	1982	1983	1984	1985	1986	1987	1988
Liabilities of the NBY (percentage change)	45.0	34.6	52.1	74.4	62.6	59.5	70.4	186.3	217.5
of which: (percentage contribution) Autonomous factors									
Selective credits	9.8	13.7	11.5	9.2	6.7	7.5	5.1	13.8	14.0
Specific credits	7.8	9.5	9.5	7.3	2.6	2.1	3.2	1.5	1.1
Other[1]	19.6	6.3	30.7	52.7	42.8	41.0	45.5	141.6	173.6
Discretionary factors	7.8	5.1	0.4	5.2	10.5	8.9	16.6	29.4	28.8

1. Essentially valuation effects.
Source: National Bank of Yugoslavia, *Quarterly Bulletin.*

the rediscount of selective credits under the pressure of regional authorities (Table 12). The second channel of autonomous central-bank money creation has been a consequence of the take-over by the NBY of exchange-rate-induced increases in banks' dinar liabilities mainly *vis-à-vis* households in possession of foreign-exchange deposits, and of the extra costs arising from these increases. As discussed above, this has been tantamount to an involuntary subsidisation of the banking system or the economy as a whole with negative implications for the allocation of credits and the growth of money supply, notably in periods when there was a need for tight monetary policies.

There is also a lack of automatic stabilisers and limited scope for discretionary corrective action in the fiscal and budgetary domain. The balanced-budget principle to be observed at all levels of government and administration calls for procyclical adjustments of expenditure and/or receipts. However, the elasticity of revenues with respect to changes in income and activity levels is close to unity, reflecting the high weight of flat-rate contributions and indirect taxes in total revenue. Similarly, social transfer payments are not particularly responsive to changes in the business cycle as reduced demand for labour in a large measure translates into labour hoarding in enterprises and a rising number of "discouraged workers"; moreover, unemployment benefits are not particularly high and the share of beneficiaries in total unemployment is relatively low.

The role of public finance to smooth the evolution of demand automatically or to allow the possibility of a discretionary change is further restricted by the small size of the Federal budget relative to that of lower levels of government and the lack of co-ordination between different administrative units, which also reduces public sector efficiency. Federal receipts in terms of GSP were on average only slightly above 6 per cent in the second half of the 1980s, lower than in any of the decentralised OECD countries. Moreover, the bulk of federal revenue is made up of customs duties and general sales taxes, i.e. of sources of revenue which are notoriously unsuitable for demand-management purposes, in particular for combating inflation.

Structural reforms

Reforms prior to 1988

Since the establishment of the Economic Stabilisation Commission in 1982, the authorities have recurrently reassessed policies and objectives. Along with

45

measures to redress the balance-of-payments situation, successive stabilisation programmes have stressed the need for the adoption of market-oriented reforms. The reform process was slow to start and reforms were introduced in a piecemeal fashion until 1988. This reflected the difficulties in reconciling conflicting regional interests, changing long-ingrained mentalities and behaviour and reducing political interference, especially at local and regional levels. Moreover, the number of trained people capable of monitoring and implementing the reforms was limited and certain of the proposed reforms failed to address the right issues or even weakened competitive forces.

After 1984, a number of laws were passed aimed at strengthening financial discipline of enterprises. The measures taken included wage cuts for loss-making and/or illiquid enterprises, reduction in subsidies and the speeding-up of bankruptcy procedures. Inflation-cost accounting was introduced in 1987, a long-overdue measure for a high-inflation country. However, financial discipline of enterprises does not appear to have improved much over the last five years or so, probably because they continue to receive financial support, including concealed subsidies by local political bodies and banks. Moreover, infringements of rules did not give rise to effective sanctions. Nor does the shift from historic to inflation-cost accounting appear to have had any significant impact on enterprises' behaviour. This may in part have been due to technical difficulties in calculating replacement costs in periods of runaway inflation. For the same reason and owing to distortions in relative prices the application of economic and social rates of return for evaluating investment projects, notably in infrastructure, has not progressed much since its introduction in the mid-1980s.

The 1987 Bank Law was an important step towards the consolidation of the banking sector and the adoption of a real-interest-rate policy. The law has made inflation-accounting obligatory so that banks could no longer hide real losses by running down the real value of equity and reserves or net assets in their balance sheets. In order to raise the extra funds required for preserving the real value of own capital, banks were, in line with the legislators' intentions, compelled to increase real lending rates significantly. However, this was achieved mainly by imposing very high real interest rates on healthy enterprises (sometimes in excess of 30 per cent). In contrast, real interest rates on loans to loss-making enterprises remained low and banks frequently wrote-off part of these loans to ensure the survival of these enterprises. At the same time banks had every incentive to keep interest rates on deposits as low as possible. In this they were helped by the geographical cartelisation of the banking sector, the related absence of competition for deposits and the lack of alternative financial instruments for asset holders.

Combined with accelerated inflation this largely explains the difficulties in establishing real positive interest rates for deposits.

The 1986-87 modest import liberalisation steps (mainly by shifting certain goods from the quota system to more liberal regimes) were nullified by the shortage of convertible currency receipts and the consequent rationing of foreign exchange. By contrast, the policy-induced gradual reduction of trade on a clearing basis has strengthened competitive forces, though less than might have been expected. Restrictions on foreign investment were eased between 1984 and 1986, notably concerning the maximum foreign share in joint-ventures and the repatriation of profits. However, foreign direct investment responded little to these measures, reflecting more fundamental obstacles associated with self-management and the related ambiguities regarding ownership and ownership rights. As a result, between 1967, when foreign investments were first allowed, and 1988 net foreign investment amounted to less than half a billion US dollars cumulatively, i.e. less than what was invested in Spain in an average month between 1986 and 1988.

The new market-oriented reform programme since 1988

a) Reform of the enterprise sector

The February 1989 *Act on Financial Operations* of enterprises replaced and simplified the previous system of rehabilitation of firms. In order to avoid problems arising from the evaluation of enterprise losses, the liquidity position has become the main criterion for assessing the viability of a company. An enterprise is declared "insolvent" if actual resources are considered by the SDK as being insufficient to cover expenditures. In the absence of a rehabilitation agreement between the insolvent enterprise and its creditors, the SDK initiates bankruptcy procedures. In 1989, one firm out of fifteen, involving half a million workers, was declared insolvent by the SDK. However, bankruptcy procedures have been opened for less than a fifth of such insolvent enterprises. This may be explained by local political pressure and the reluctance of creditors to engage in bankruptcy procedures, as they do not come first in the schedule of attribution of bankruptcy proceeds. The law on obligatory liquidation of enterprises passed in December 1989 has made local authorities responsible for the assessment of enterprises' viability. Henceforth, it is up to the local authorities to decide upon a rehabilitation or a liquidation of an enterprise on the basis of an analysis of the balance sheets by independent experts.

The *Enterprises Law*, adopted in December 1988, stipulates the unification of management within socialised enterprises. Thus, effective as of January 1990, the semi-independent sub-units of enterprises (BOALs) have been suppressed. More importantly, the new law allows the creation of enterprises with all types of ownership, including wholly privately-owned and co-operatives. Also, a wide variety of legal forms of enterprises has been introduced: firstly, within the private sector, a distinction is made between unincorporated enterprises, limited partnership and shareholding companies. Secondly, within the socialised sector, joint companies can now be created by two or more socially-owned enterprises. Finally, the law permits the acquisition of a share (or the total) of the equity of a socialised enterprise by a private company, although the procedures to be followed have not yet been clearly established. Also, the role and rights of workers' councils in private or "mixed" enterprises is not explicitly specified.

The Law on social capital (the *Social Capital Circulation and Management Law*), adopted in December 1989, should facilitate the transformation of socially-owned enterprises into other social or mixed-ownership companies. Local authorities in charge of rehabilitation programmes, are now in the position to oblige loss-making enterprises to sell their social capital. More importantly, the workers' council of any socially-owned firm may decide to sell part or the whole of the enterprise capital. Other socially-owned firms, as well as private companies (both domestic and foreign) and individuals (including the workers of the firm) can purchase shares of the enterprise without any restrictions. Proceeds from such sales accrue to a special public agency. The law stipulates that in each republic and autonomous province there should be one such agency[16]. By recognising the importance of management rights of capital owners the law should serve to pave the way for a gradual transformation of parts of the socialised sector into mixed or private ownership in a competitive environment.

The extent to which the possibilities offered by the various laws related to the organisation and operation of enterprises will be fully exploited as a vehicle to inject more dynamism into the economic system through private entrepreneurship and capital-based technical know-how or innovative processes remains to be seen. Given the size of the socialised sector on the one hand and the limited availability of investible funds on the part of the general public on the other, the transformation of social capital into other forms of ownership will inevitably take time. The present law on social capital, while no doubt an important step forward in this direction, however, does not address or remove all problems related to the absence of well-defined property and management rights and the associated lack of competitive behaviour. First, for its application the consent and the co-operation of regional and local governments is required which cannot always be taken for granted. Secondly, there are a few incentives for workers of viable, well-performing, enterprises to "go private". This means that for a large part of the socialised sector both the workers' interests and the interests of the anonymous capital owners will continue to be represented by labour i.e. – contrary to optimal solutions of conflict situations – solely by one party, namely the user of capital[17]. Thirdly, the interest of an enterprise or private investor, notably a foreign one, in acquiring another company or a share of it will be negatively affected as long as the relevant laws fail to specify unambiguously the extent to which management powers will have to be shared with, or will be restricted by, the workers' council.

b) *Reform of the banking sector*

Since June 1989, the competences and autonomy of the NBY have been enlarged. While monetary targets will continue to be fixed ultimately by the Federal Assembly, the Bank has been given the right to submit its proposals to the Assembly. Moreover, most decisions of the National Bank's board can now be taken by a simple majority instead of the previously required unanimity, and the Governor can veto any decisions and submit the unsettled issue to the Assembly.

The National Bank's control over money supply has also been, or will be, significantly improved. First, the long-standing practice of selective (subsidised) crediting is to be discontinued and any subsidisation of "priority sectors" will have to be done through the budget. Secondly, liquidity credits to commercial banks will no longer be granted on simple request but are subject to a prior credit-worthiness evaluation by the NBY. Thirdly, central bank credits to the Federation now require authorisation by the Federal Assembly. Another change which should serve to curb central-bank money growth arises from the government's decisions that the losses from hedging operations against dinar devaluations conducted since 1978 between the NBY and the commercial banks and any new losses from such operations have to be borne and serviced by the federal budget.

Apart from enlarged competence and better command over monetary growth, the central bank's prudential control powers over the banking sector have also been significantly strengthened by the Law on the rehabilitation of banks, adopted in December 1989. Solvency ratios have been imposed by the NBY, limiting the total amount of assets to less than fifteen times the equity. In order to reduce exposure to risk, ceilings on foreign credits and long-term credits have also been introduced. Moreover, the NBY has been made responsible for the attribution of bank licences. Banks have presented a plan to the NBY of how to comply by 1991 with the new solvency ratios. The NBY may initiate rehabilitation procedures, if losses exceed permanent bank resources (equity plus reserves). A bank can be rehabilitated by way of new investments in the bank, partial or complete write-off of claims, take-over of certain losses and liabilities of the bank, and the sale of shares to other entities. A bank can be rehabilitated only to the extent that its bankruptcy is liable to affect other agents, notably creditors of the bank. Hence, if creditors of a loss-making bank are not interested in its rehabilitation, the NBY may institute bank-ruptcy procedures.

The rehabilitation of banks is undertaken by a newly-created special federal agency, under the supervision of the NBY (December 1989 law on the federal agency for the rehabilitation of the banking system). In principle, all banks have to insure their deposits with the agency, so that in case of illiquidity or liquidation, the agency takes over these deposits. However, given that the agency will have to take over certain initial bank losses, the insurance premiums paid by banks are unlikely to cover the rehabilitation costs of the agency. Therefore, funds from the federal budget have been allocated to this agency, which can also issue dinar bonds.

According to the new banking law, adopted in February 1989, banks have to be transformed into shareholding companies. This is opening the possibility for new investors, including private investors, to enlarge the equity base of the banks. However, individuals have no voting rights, which remain confined to the founding members (enterprises) of the bank. Bank shares, notably from loss-makers, are therefore unlikely to become attractive financial investment outlets. Moreover, the risk that banks continue to discriminate in their lending conditions in favour of founding members, and notably big debtors, remains. In particular, the financial impediments to the creation of new companies and the provision of venture capital have not been removed. It would therefore seem important that new investors be given full voting rights corresponding to their share capital. Greater competition between banks would also help to enhance the intermediation role of the financial system. The recent bank law enables enterprises to open giro accounts with differ-ent banks, but in practice few firms have yet done so. This may be taken as an indication of insufficient inter-bank competition. Therefore, the establishment of new private and foreign banks should be encouraged, perhaps by way of fiscal incentives. Also, the establishment of a nation-wide capital market, accessible to all Yugoslav share-holding companies, could prove useful. It could help the rehabilita-tion process for banks and enterprises alike. The recently-created money and security markets in Belgrade, Zagreb and Ljubljana do not play this role, since it is reserved for banks.

c) *Liberalisation of imports, foreign-exchange transactions and direct foreign investment*

Import liberalisation was a key element of the May 1988 stabilisation package and the associated standby arrangements with the IMF. Aided by the comfortable balance-of-payments position, import liberalisation has proceeded at a fast pace so that by the end of 1989 only 13 per cent of goods remained subject to quotas compared with 46 per cent two years earlier. The conditionally-free import regime (i.e. imports tied to the availability of foreign exchange) and licences were abolished, entailing a spectacular increase in the share of goods under the free-import regime from 10 per cent at the end of 1987 to 87 per cent only two years later (Table 13). Moreover, the right to import of socialised enterprises has been

Table 13. **Import liberalisation**

	31.12.87	30.6.88	31.12.88	11.3.89	8.4.89	6.8.89	19.8.89	31.8.89	15.9.89
Free imports	10.0	44.3	55.0	64.7	69.0	77.5	83.5	86.5	87.0
Conditionally[1] free imports	42.0	33.3	27.3	17.9	14.0	8.0	3.0	0.0	0.0
Quotas	45.6	21.1	17.7	17.4	17.0	14.5	13.5	13.5	13.0
Licences	2.4	1.3	0.0	0.0	0.0	0.0	0.0	0.0	0.0
Total[2]	100	100	100	100	100	100	100	100	100

1. Depending on the availability of foreign exchange.
2. Import weights have been derived from 1988 trade values.
Source: Data submitted by national authorities.

extended to private companies and for certain consumer goods to individuals as well. This represents an important break with the past of more than 40 years of heavy protection – a record which has led to important distortions not only with regard to trade flows but also with respect to production patterns and regional location of activities. The extent to which restrictions on foreign trade have been removed is overstated by the figures shown in Table 13 and the effective protection of several sectors of the economy is still relatively high[18].

Together with the trade liberalisation measures in May 1988 the system of administrative allocation of foreign exchange was abolished and a "unified" foreign-exchange market, covering Yugoslavia as a whole, was established in the second half of 1988. This interbank market operates under the supervision of the NBY. The NBY determines daily its intervention rate on the basis of commercial banks' submissions of their transaction plans and their projections for the next three days. The exchange rate used for direct transactions between participating banks is linked to the NBY intervention rate, i.e. the rate at which the NBY is willing to sell or buy the balance left after all direct transactions between banks have been concluded. Most of the authorised banks participating in the market are regionally-based associate banks. Only after having acted as clearing houses for their member banks do they enter the unified market for the residual demand or supply of foreign exchange. Accordingly, the turnover of the market is relatively small. In 1989, it totalled less than $3 billion or one-fourth of total trade in goods and services in convertible currencies. With a share of about two-thirds of the total value of transactions, the NBY holds a dominant position in the market. In contrast to the previous foreign-exchange allocation system, which had produced a multiple of shadow exchange rates by linking import rights of a republic or province to its respective export earnings, there is only one exchange rate under the present system applying to all convertible-currency transactions of all regions. This ensures a better allocation of resources in Yugoslavia as a whole, notably by facilitating the development of export-oriented activities.

Appreciable progress has also been made to decontrol foreign investment. The new Foreign Investment Law of 1st January 1989 is considerably more liberal than its predecessors. In line with the market-oriented spirit of the new enterprise law introduced at the same time (see above), different types of ownership and related management rights can now be acquired by foreign investors. Both foreign companies and private persons can set up a wholly-owned company or enter into partnership with local companies or with private persons. These companies can take the form of joint-stock companies, limited liability companies, limited or unlimited partnership etc. Management rights are shared according to the capital provided. In contrast to the previous provisions there are no longer any time limits fixed to the duration of foreign investments. Rules concerning repatriation of capital and profits as well as capital guarantees have been aligned to common OECD practices and the procedure for foreign-investment approvals has also been simplified. In addition, a law for the creation of "free custom zones" was passed recently, granting important tax privileges to companies which establish themselves or subsidiaries in these zones. The main conditions to be fulfilled are that at least 70 per cent of the goods and services produced must be exported and these exports must exceed $30 million per annum.

In the first year after the introduction of the foreign investment law there was a surge in applications[19]. About two-thirds were for the creation of joint ventures with local companies and the rest equally divided between the establishment of single-owned new companies and investment in existing ones, notably in enterprises with which foreign companies had been maintaining long-term contracts of co-operation. Despite this surge, the total amount involved did not exceed DM 600 million[20]. Indeed, the average foreign investment was only DM 1.17 million; the biggest single project amounted to DM 3.1 million and the average of the smallest 25 per cent of all investment projects was not more than DM 5 000. Most foreign investment went to the service sector (tourism, entertainment, restaurants and shops) and little to industry. Slovenia followed by Croatia received the highest proportion of foreign investment in per capita terms. Macedonia, Bosnia and Herzegovinia and Kosovo together captured less than one-fifth of the total. Germany, Italy and Austria accounted for more than one-half of the value of foreign investment, other EC countries some 7 per cent and the United States about 14 per cent.

d) *Liberalisation of prices*

After nearly half a century of an extended system of administrative price controls, the lifting of these controls was a *conditio sine qua non* for the whole reform process. As from mid-1988, prices have been progressively liberalised. By September 1989, only a few prices remained subject to controls or were still officially fixed (Table 14). In theory, the authorities maintained control over a large number of prices under two regimes: "cost-linked automatic price increases" (i.e. mark-up cost pricing) and "prices based on common elements" (i.e. on inputs, world prices and/or certain other reference prices). However, as the authorities did not have the means to check effectively the validity of all the justifications for price rises presented to them, in practice enterprises have enjoyed wide powers in setting prices, with the exception of public utilities. The abolition of all indirect price controls at the end of December 1989, the simultaneous transfer of the products concerned back under the direct control of the Federal government and the freezing for six months of one-fourth of prices were key elements of the anti-inflation programme, and as such should be seen as a temporary measure (see Part III). Moreover, it should be noted that, despite this backward step, at the end of 1989 some 75 per cent of all prices covered by the industrial producer index (and about the same percentage for the retail price index) were freely determined, compared with some 40 per cent at the end of 1987.

Despite the favourable effects which can be expected to flow from recent reforms, the price and import liberalisation measures cannot be expected by themselves to ensure the disappearance of excessive regional price disparities. The elimination of nationalistic tendencies in individual republics and provinces would,

53

Table 14. Price control regime since 1987
Industrial producer prices

	1987					1988				1989						
	Jan.-Mar	Apr.-June	July	Aug.-Oct.	Nov.	28th May	Aug.	Sept.	Nov.	Jan.	Mar.	Apr.	May	Sept.	Oct.	Dec.
Administered prices decided by the Federal Executive Council	8.5	14.7	14.7	11.3	100.0	22.0	9.2	2.2	2.2	4.4	3.7	3.2	–	–	23.2	24.3
Prices approved by the Federal Bureau of Prices (FBP)	26.5	26.5	26.9	26.9	–	14.3	14.3	11.9	2.8	2.8	2.6	2.2	2.2	0.7	0.7	0.6
Price changes subject to pre-notification to the FBP[1]	8.7	8.7	5.0	5.0	–	–	–	–	–	–	–	–	–	–	–	–
Buyers and FBP given thirty days advance notice	8.9	8.9	12.2	12.2	–	16.2	16.2	16.2	–	12.8	13.4	13.4	13.4	13.0	1.1	–
Cost-linked automatic price increases	4.9	3.5	3.5	3.0	–	0.4	0.4	7.7	11.7	9.0	9.3	9.3	12.6	12.6	–	–
Prices based on common elements	–	–	–	–	–	–	12.8	12.8	12.8	–	–	–	–	–	–	–
Freely-determined prices	**42.5**	**37.7**	**37.8**	**41.6**	**–**	**47.1**	**47.1**	**49.2**	**70.5**	**71.0**	**71.0**	**71.8**	**71.8**	**73.8**	**75.1**	**75.1**
Total	100.0	100.0	100.0	100.0	100.0	100.0	100.0	100.0	100.0	100.0	100.0	100.0	100.0	100.0	100.0	100.0

Note: For details on price control regimes since 1982 see OECD Economic Survey of Yugoslavia, Annex I, January 1987 and Annex I, 1987-88.

1. Until June 1986 the pre-notification period was 30 days. On 25th June 1986 this was prolonged to 120 days and in November 1986 was changed to 90 days.

Source: Federal Bureau of Prices.

of course, greatly facilitate this task. In addition, it is important to establish a legal framework and federal institutions which are responsible for implementing competition policies. These institutions should have extensive powers of control and to impose fines not only on individual companies or groups of enterprises, but also on lower levels of government. The latter through biased procurement bids, hidden subsidies and pricing policies discriminate against enterprises not located in their own territory.

The unification of tradeable goods and services in a single Yugoslav market will, likewise, continue to be impeded by the fragmented transportation and telecommunications systems. Railway and telecommunications companies are confined to republics. They act as if they were part of a cartel, in which each company has carved out a part of the Yugoslav market without having to fear competition from others. The absence of a real national road network under the responsibility of the Federal government, at least for trans-Yugoslav highways, has also served to reinforce the segmentation of markets. Indeed, motorways spring out from the capitals of certain republics to other main cities of the same republic (or to some of its foreign neighbours), but usually are not connected with those of other republics. Needless to say, this has negative effects on travel time and the cost of transport in Yugoslavia as a whole.

e) Consolidation of public finance

The consolidation of the public-sector accounts has made good progress since the middle of 1989 following the incorporation in the Federal budget of off-budget accounts and of the NBY's dinar-devaluation losses arising from its uncovered foreign-exchange liabilities *vis-à-vis* the commercial banks. Cumulated losses during the 1980s amounted to about US$10 billion or 17 per cent of 1989 GSP. For the first time the interest payments on foreign-exchange deposits, mainly of households, will in 1990 be borne by the federal budget (estimated at $500 million). Similarly, the selective-credit subsidy will be paid out of the federal budget. Its estimated cost is $250 million in 1990. A roughly equal sum is earmarked in the 1990 federal budget for the rehabilitation of banks and for social expenses associated with the restructuring of the enterprise sector. In all, these additional outlays are officially expected to increase Federal government expenditure by some $1 billion or nearly 2 per cent of GSP.

In order to speed up the integration of off-budget accounts at the lower levels of government as well, a constitutional amendment has recently been proposed by the Federal Executive Council to pave the way for the suppression or the merger of a large number of the more than 5 000 independent self-managed communities of interest (for education, health, social welfare, housing, for infrastructure works, etc.) and the transfer of parts of their functions and budgets to republics, provinces and/or municipalities. Consolidation is not only expected to increase transparency and cost-efficiency of spending programmes and revenue collection but should also reinforce the control of higher over lower levels of government, thereby promoting coherence and consistency of fiscal policy across the whole territory of Yugoslavia.

Other constitutional amendments, which are under active consideration, aim at completing the market-oriented fiscal reforms by 1995. The most important tax change envisaged is the introduction of VAT in 1994. Tarification of import quotas is also planned and should be realised over the next couple of years. The imposition of import duties on a large number of products, which were up to now subject to non-price rationing devices but exempt from taxation, will help to raise tax revenues and, even more importantly, will be less discriminatory than quotas and licences. Both on equity and fiscal grounds, personal income-tax yields are planned to be increased in 1991. The proposals include the taxation of income which has so far been effectively excluded from taxation (income from agriculture and from other private sector activities including real-estate income), higher tax rates on high incomes and the taxation of households rather than individual income earners.

The Federal Government has also submitted proposals to reduce distortions that arise from major differences in taxation between republics, provinces and within certain regions. The harmonisation of taxation would also help delineate better the administrative competence of the various levels of government, thus preventing unnecessary conflicts and enhancing public-sector efficiency. Under the project, now being examined, the Federal Government will be responsible for laying down the basic rules regarding the definition of the tax base and the regulation of tax exemptions. It will also fix ranges for certain tax rates while the actual rates to be applied are to remain under the responsibility of the republican or provincial authorities. Although these proposals provide a flexible framework and involve only limited surrender of power by the republics and provinces, their acceptance still faces great difficulties.

f) *Social policies and the labour market*

The transition towards a market economy and the consequent opening-up of domestic markets to greater external and internal competition will lead to the liquidations of uncompetitive enterprises and shifts of resources to more profitable activities. This transformation process will inevitably be accompanied by higher unemployment and social costs. The obligation for enterprises to add to their workforce qualified new entrants into the labour marked[21] has already been lifted and lay-offs have been made easier since the introduction of the new labour law of 1989. Rough official estimates put the overmanning in industry at nearly one-fifth of total employment in the socialised sector. This overstates the extent to which the number of jobless people may temporarily rise since the dynamic employment-creation effects of restructuring must also be taken into consideration. Nevertheless, on balance it seems prudent to reckon with a substantial rise in unemployment during the restructuring period. In order to keep the associated social costs politically manageable, the authorities have opted for a gradualist approach aimed at eliminating overmanning by the mid-1990s.

First steps have been taken to establish a social safety net for redundant workers on a nation-wide scale. The 1990 Federal budget has earmarked some $150 million as financial support for social programmes in the republics and provinces[22]. An additional $100 million is expected to be provided by the budgets of republics and provinces. The federal fund, though still small in size, is to help finance the labour-market assistance programmes in those republics and provinces which do not have sufficient means of their own. As restructuring will affect mainly the underdeveloped regions, the latter will be the main recipients of federal funds. The authorities also plan to give a lump sum amounting to a minimum of two years' wages for persons wishing to establish themselves as self-employed. In 1989 the "Federal bureau for employment", in co-operation with the employment services in the republics and provinces made considerable progress in establishing a modern and comprehensive unified information system. Its main goal is to collect and diffuse information regarding employment offers and needs emanating from each regional employment office to the rest of the offices located in other parts of Yugoslavia.

The above policies do not, however, directly tackle some of the more deep-seated roots of existing labour-market rigidities: regional market segmentation, the lack of labour demand and supply adjustments to changing macro and microeconomic conditions, and insufficient wage differentiation as between different skills and efficiency levels. This implies that the favourable economy-wide effects of the recent reforms will inevitably be more limited. The authorities and the public at large have for long under-rated the importance of a competent class of managers and technicians with a "corporate mentality". Managers, appointed by local politicians or by workers and working under the threat of being dismissed if they do not give in to the demands of these two powerful pressure groups, cannot exercise their functions properly and establish targets for production, employment and wages on a realistic basis. A related issue is the strong compression of pay differentials (Table 15). This demotivates higher-educated and skilled personnel, who often try to increase their incomes by fraudulent practices or doing other jobs. Over and above the short-term negative consequences, insufficient remuneration of competence and talent as well as the fact that pay differentials barely cover the cost of education (including foregone wages) leads over time to supply bottlenecks in certain skills with adverse implications for the growth potential of the Yugoslav economy. It remains to be seen whether the recent decision to introduce free-wage bargaining in the second half of 1990 will improve the wage structure significantly. For the moment labour unions are supposed to negotiate with chambers of commerce whose representatives are primarily managers of enterprises appointed by workers' councils.

Table 15. **Wage differentials**
Average wage of an unskilled worker = 100

	1976	1986
Wages according to skill level		
Without qualifications	100	100
Semi-qualified	110	111
Average qualifications	130	126
Highly-qualified	175	156
Wages according to educational level		
Primary school	120	104
Secondary school	152	138
Higher education	188	172
University degree	253	218

Source: Federal Statistical Office, *Annual Yearbook of Yugoslavia*, 1989.

The creation in 1989 of a unified nation-wide information system regarding employment opportunities, should help to improve horizontal mobility. However, if the "inward-looking" tendencies of regional employment offices are to be overcome, the Federal Office should have greater responsibilities in the sphere of co-ordination and not just be limited to the diffusion of (selective) information provided by the regional employment offices. Likewise, the absence of a well-functioning rental market for housing is an important obstacle to labour mobility. Heavily-subsidised rents established by enterprises and local authorities on the one hand, and unduly-high rents in the much smaller private rental market on the other, cannot but discourage mobility. Fostering geographical as well as skill mobility and assisting workers in job searching will therefore make for an important contribution of public employment offices.

g) *Completing the reform process*

Important progress has been made during the last couple of years in lifting impediments to a proper functioning of markets and to better economic management on both the enterprise and the public sector level. However, in some key areas the reforms have further to go. Banks continue to be effectively run by the founding enterprises i.e. the main debtors; and the resulting misallocation of national savings is compounded by the fact that banks remain virtually the sole financial intermediaries. Moreover, ownership rights in socialised and mixed enterprises have not clearly been established so that the distribution of income may continue to be biased against savings. Another systemic weakness not yet tackled by reforms is the extremely weak constitutional power of the federal authorities. This is reflected in an inappropriate fiscal structure (both for the pursuit of supply-side goals and for demand management purposes), the persisting exposure of the NBY to regional political pressure and last but not least effective anti-competition barriers between republics and provinces.

III. Stabilisation measures and short-term prospects

The December 1989 stabilisation measures and the present policy environment

Towards the end of 1989 the authorities became increasingly preoccupied with the runaway inflation, its pervasive economic effects and the risks it posed to the implementation of institutional and structural reforms. The size of the problems had called for severe and sweeping measures. In mid-December 1989 a comprehensive anti-inflation package was introduced. It included a timed wage and partial price freeze coupled with an exchange-rate-guarantee clause and other administrative controls up to the end of June 1990. Within this period the authorities expected inflation to be brought under firm control. In addition, restrictive fiscal and monetary targets for 1990 were adopted. These measures were projected to reduce the rate of inflation from 2 700 per cent during 1989 to 13 per cent during 1990, with real wages falling by some 2.5 per cent in 1990 as a whole. A decline in private and government consumption and a marked slowdown in stockbuilding were also expected, entailing in conjunction with continuing increases in real net merchandise imports a fall in GSP of some 2 per cent in 1990. The weakening of the real foreign balance is officially projected to translate into a shrinking of the current-account surplus from 3 per cent of GSP in 1989 to 2 per cent in 1990.

The anti-inflation package announced on 19th December 1989 comprised the following measures:

i) Introduction of a new currency unit with one new dinar equalling 10 000 old dinars;

ii) The new dinar was made convertible and pegged to the Deutschemark (DM) at an exchange rate of 1 DM = 7 new dinars guaranteed during the period of the wage freeze[23];

iii) Imposition of a wage stop with wages to be frozen up to the end of June at their level as of the 15th December 1989 (pertaining to wages paid out

Table 16. **Government targets for 1990**

Percentage change at constant 1985 prices

	1988		1989		1990
	Resolution	Outcome	Resolution	Outcome[1]	Targets
Private consumption	0.5	–1.3	1.8	1.0	–0.5
Public consumption	–3.2	0.1	–0.1	–1.0	–2.0
Fixed investment	2.5	–5.8	3.5	0.5	2.0
Final domestic demand	0.6	–2.2	2.4	0.6	–
Total domestic demand	0.0	–1.1	–	–1.1	–
Foreign balance	–1.8	1.1	–	–1.1	–
Exports	5.4	5.7	5.1	7.2	8.0
Imports	12.4	1.1	8.2	12.7	16.0
Statistical discrepancy	3.9	–1.7	–	–3.3	–
Social product	2.0	–1.7	1.5	0.8	–2.0
of which:					
Agriculture	4.0	–3.3	6.0	3.6	2.0
Industry	2.0	–0.7	1.0	1.8	–2.0
Memorandum items:					
Current external balance in convertible					
currencies ($ billion)	(0.4)	(2.2)	(1.6)	(2.0)	(1.4)
Socialised sector					
Employment	1.0	0.0	0.5	–0.4	–
Productivity	0.8	–1.6	0.6	0.8	–
of which:					
Industry	1.0	–1.1	0.4	0.9	–
Real net average earnings[2]	–0.5	–8.0	0.6	6.5	–2.5

1. Provisional estimates.
2. Official data based on the period to which wages pertain and not OECD estimates (see Table 1) which show when wages are actually paid.
Source: Federal Planning Office.

for the month of November) and to be maintained stable in DM terms over this period. However, for many wage earners, who had suffered big real wage losses in the previous few months, wages were allowed to be raised by up to 20 per cent. Likewise, wages more than 20 per cent below the republican or provincial average could be raised to the 80 per cent level. These two adjustments were officially estimated to raise average wages by 15 per cent in January 1990 over December;

iv) Imposition of a partial six-month price freeze as of 1st January affecting 25 per cent of industrial producer goods, notably public utilities, ferrous and non-ferrous metals and pharmaceuticals. The freeze was preceded by considerable upward price adjustments in the course of December which had been aimed at reducing distortions in the structure of prices. In addition, a price stop was decreed for rents and other housing charges, mainly levied by local authorities.

The Federal Government reaffirmed its resolve to maintain a tough macroeconomic policy stance. The more effective control over money supply which the NBY is now able to exercise and the non-inflationary financing of various public-sector deficits should help in this respect. The 1990 target for the growth of net domestic assets of the banking sector was fixed at 7 per cent and for M1 at 24 per cent. The NBY has given directives that bank credits should be reduced by 20 per cent during the first quarter of 1990 (NBY credits by 30 per cent) and that interest rates on dinar deposits be raised to positive real levels (ranging from 5 per cent for three-month deposits to 12 per cent for deposits of three years or more). At the same time the Bank has fixed its own discount rate at 24 per cent. To limit "autonomous" monetary growth, the NBY ruled that payments in dinars for exports on a clearing basis will not be made unless importers from the clearing area make corresponding dinar payments.

At the beginning of the year liquidity was growing considerably more than had been projected, reflecting a repatriation of foreign-exchange receipts by exporters

Table 17. **The Federal budget**

	Billion dinars		Per cent of GSP			
	1989 Outcome	1990 Budget	1987	1988	1989[1]	1990[2] Budget
Regular revenue	119 400	753 168	6.1	5.4	6.0	9.6
Customs duties	33 700	327 769	1.6	1.6	1.7	4.2
Basic sales tax	66 700	359 060	3.1	2.9	3.4	4.6
Contributions from republics and provinces	15 700	59 320	1.2	0.8	0.8	0.8
Other	3 200	7 019	0.1	0.1	0.2	0.0
Expenditure	108 300	695 109	6.0	5.4	5.5	8.9
Defence	61 100	347 895	4.0	3.8	3.1	4.5
Administration	12 700	61 439	0.4	0.5	0.6	0.8
Grants to republics and provinces	7 000	35 401	0.3	0.3	0.4	0.5
Investment	600	19 535	0.0	0.0	0.0	0.2
Grants to pension funds	11 100	31 566	1.1	0.8	0.6	0.4
Other	15 800	199 272	0.0	0.0	0.8	2.5
Balance on regular account	11 100	58 060	0.0	0.0	0.6	0.7
Financial transactions						
Budget reserves	4	39 177				
Debt repayments and other	725	18 883				

Note: Data may no add due to rounding.
1. Based on official estimates for GSP.
2. Based on official projections, see Table 16.
Source: Data submitted by national authorities.

after the December stabilisation measures, increases in households' deposits and high end-year interest receipts. In February, to contain the increase in liquidity the NBY instructed commercial banks to invest 700 million dinars in NBY bills with an interest rate two-fifths below the NBY discount rate. On the other hand, to prevent a squeeze on bank profits, the NBY raised the interest rate paid on obligatory reserves from 12 to 25 per cent.

It is also planned to keep the stance of fiscal policy restrictive for the second year running. As already discussed in the context of budgetary reforms in Part II, the incorporation of off-budget items and extra expenditure by the public sector (for the rehabilitation of banks, the strengthening of the social safety net for redundant workers, for interest payments on foreign-exchange deposits and for subsidising selective credits) is officially estimated to cost some 3 per cent of GSP, the greatest part of which (some 80 per cent) will be covered by increased taxation. Accordingly, the Federal government imposed a special turnover tax of 3 per cent applying to all products, excluding food products, and of 5 per cent to a great number of services (banks, insurance companies, trading companies, etc.) that were previously exempted[24]. The tarification of import quotas is also expected to increase considerably customs revenues accruing to the Federal budget. As the underdeveloped regions are expected to be the principal beneficiaries of the extra budgetary expenditure mentioned above, it was decided to limit the transfers to underdeveloped regions through the Federal fund for underdeveloped regions to some 0.5 per cent of GSP in 1990.

Concerned about the inflationary effects of certain practices followed in 1989, the authorities took measures to prevent enterprises from including doubtful financial claims as realised revenues out of which wages are being paid. Likewise, the authorities announced that controls by the SDK will be strengthened so that enterprises recording substantial profits after the completion of their final accounts in March will also be prevented from increasing their wage bill in real terms. However, these enterprises have the possibility of distributing these profits in the form of bonds and shares to their workers after the end of June 1990 or may be allowed to increase wages if this is matched by a corresponding decrease in the number of workers. The authorities were also concerned about a possible upward drift of some essential food prices, e.g. bread and meat, which could immediately trigger off inflation expectations. To dissuade local monopolies and relevant enterprises from abusing dominant market positions the authorities announced that if deemed necessary they would impose special price controls on these categories of goods.

The anti-inflation strategy

Against the background of the 1989 inflation record, the price and balance-of-payments targets for 1990 seem at first sight extremely optimistic and the decision to peg the weak dinar to one of the hardest currencies in the world untenable. Firstly, because the sharply-accelerating pace of inflation during 1989 and the 15 per cent wage rise accorded in January 1990 suggest that there are still important price pressures "in the pipeline". Secondly, convertibility combined with a guaranteed exchange rate for a fixed period in the face of still high price rises by international comparison in the early months of the year could induce a shift out of dinars into foreign currencies towards the end of the wage freeze and steepen import growth. Under these conditions the balance-of-payments position could come under considerable strain with downward pressure on the exchange rate building up. The authorities are conscious of these risks, but count on countervailing forces, such as favourable supply-side effects of the reforms discussed in Part II, foreign financial backing and moral support for the reforms. The authorities also reckon with continued relatively rapid growth in Yugoslavia's main export markets and a quick build-up of domestic confidence when first positive results of the stabilisation and consolidation measures occur.

The starting conditions at the end of 1989 for implementing the December package were not unfavourable. Official reserves had reached a record level of $6 billion. Moreover, following the continuous acquisition of foreign currencies, household liquidity in dinars had been reduced considerably so that the margin for shifting out of dinars was limited. It was officially estimated that the potential conversion of dinars to foreign exchange by households could amount to $1.5 billion at most, leaving ample official reserves to meet fast-rising import growth. It was expected that the projected sluggishness of domestic demand and tight monetary policy will combine with better financial discipline of enterprises and growing foreign competition to exert a powerful damping impact on inflation. The authorities expected still relatively big, though sharply decelerating, price increases in the first two months, followed by a small fall in March, before inflation settles on a moderate path of around 1 per cent per month.

The pegging of the convertible dinar to the DM was prompted by the growing recognition that the inflation spiral through ever-rising inflation expectations could not be broken without establishing a solid anchor. Domestic anchors, such as those of the May 1988 anti-inflation package, had lost their credibility. The choice of the DM was appropriate as it had already gradually replaced the dinar as a unit of account for most domestic transactions over the previous twelve months and most

Diagram 10. WAGES IN FOREIGN CURRENCIES

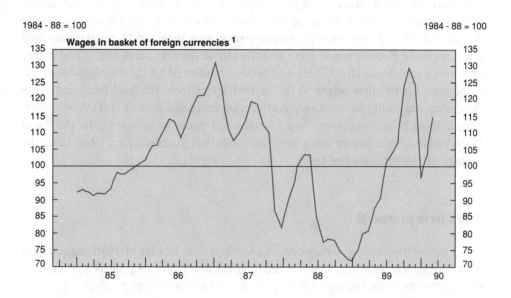

1984 - 88 = 100

Wages in basket of foreign currencies [1]

1984 - 88 = 100

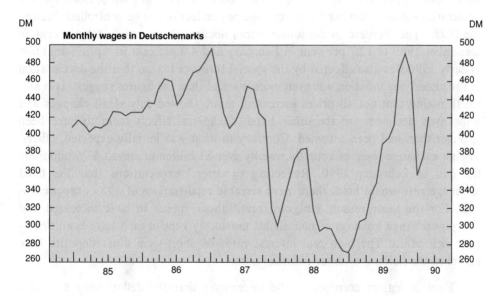

DM

Monthly wages in Deutschemarks

DM

1. Weights used are : ECU = 0.80 and US dollars 0.20.

Source : OECD estimates.

of emigrant remittances and foreign-exchange deposits are made in DM. Moreover, the commitment to maintain the exchange rate unchanged until the end of June had a twofold effect. Firstly, it signalled to enterprises that the authorities were not prepared any more to accommodate price rises by continually devaluing the dinar so that if they were to remain competitive they had to restrain cost and price increases. Secondly, and more importantly in the very short-run, it had a very favourable confidence effect. This was further reinforced by the engagement of the authorities not to allow wages to fall in DM terms from the level fixed under the December anti-inflation package. As for the exchange rate of 1 DM = 7 new dinars, though implying some loss of competitiveness as compared to 1988 and 1989, relative unit labour costs have not been left significantly higher than the average of the previous five years.

Short-term prospects

The few available statistics covering the first four months of 1990 suggest that the anti-inflation measures have started to affect developments positively, though in some areas there are important divergences from announced plans. Notably, it has been reported that the wage freeze has not been observed in some sectors, but the authorities issued directives for retroactive pay reductions to be controlled through the SDK. The increase in consumer prices declined from nearly 60 per cent in December 1989 to 12.7 per cent in February and 4.0 per cent in April[25]. Inflation in early 1990 was also affected by the special turnover tax, so that the deceleration in the underlying inflation was even more marked than the figures suggest. It is also worth noting that not all prices increased; many showed only small changes and some even declined. On the other hand, confidence effects seem to have been stronger than had been assumed. Contrary to what was initially expected, official foreign exchange reserves actually rose by over $1 billion to almost $7½ billion by the end of February 1990. Reflecting exporters' expectations that the fixed exchange rate would hold, there were sizeable repatriations of 1989 export earnings. For the same reason, emigrant remittances appear to have increased and foreign-exchange holdings of households previously kept in cash have been deposited with banks. The high real interest rates on short-term dinar deposits have favoured the holding of dinar financial assets.

Real indicators corroborate the impression that the deflationary measures have started to bite. Volume retail sales slumped by as much as 27 per cent year-on-year in the first three months of 1990 and construction activity also dropped

Table 18. **Short-term trends**

Percentage change

	1988 Dec.	1989 June	1989 Dec.	1990 Jan.	1990 Feb.	1990 March	1990 April
Industrial producer prices							
Year-to-year	273.4	787.5	2 645.1	2 733.6	2 334.3	2 048.3	1 659.4
Month-to-month	15.9	30.5	72.8	23.0	7.6	2.3	–0.2
Consumer prices							
Year-to-year	119.0	594.0	2 720.1	3 287.6	3 075.6	2 730.3	2 360.0
Month-to-month	12.9	29.0	59.8	37.6	12.7	3.8	4.4
Real wages							
Year-to-year	–5.0	14.5	5.4	–11.8	–20.2		
Month-to-month[1]	23.8	4.4	–12.0	–12.6	–16.0		
Retail sales, volume							
Year-to-year	–6.5	–10.1	–16.7	–27.0	–26.6	–25.5	
Month-to-month	7.5	–3.3	7.6	–25.0	–1.0	6.4	
Retail stocks, volume							
Year-to-year	80.5	–18.3	–37.8	–31.1	–21.5	–16.4	
Month-to-month	–1.0	–7.0	–25.1	–11.3	14.5	17.8	
Industrial production							
Year-to-year	–4.8	2.9	–9.1	–5.3	–6.1		
Month-to-month[1]	5.1	–0.3	–3.4	1.2	0.0		

	Dec. 1989 / Dec. 1988	March 1990 / March 1989	March 1990 / Dec. 1989
Currency in circulation	2 015	1 089	61.1
Dinar deposits	1 990	2 018	26.3
Foreign exchange deposits	2 377	1 597	3.4
Money supply, M2	2 325	1 755	12.1
(Real M2)	(–11)	(–36)	(–40)

	1989 Jan.–March	1989 Jan.–April	1990 Jan.–March	1990 Jan.–April
	($ million)			
Exports, total	2 918	3 948	3 505	4 892
(convertible currencies)	(2 257)	(3 032)	(2 915)	(3 957)
Imports, total	3 121	4 266	4 205	5 861
(convertible currencies)	(2 545)	(3 467)	(3 546)	(4 955)
Trade deficit	–203	–318	–700	–969
(convertible currencies)	(–288)	(–435)	(–631)	(–998)
Current account balance	29		77	
(convertible currencies)	(–96)		(97)	

1. Seasonally adjusted series.
Sources: Indeks, Federal Statistical Office, direct submission to the OECD and OECD estimates.

markedly. As a result, industrial output remained sluggish, bringing the year-to-year fall to 7 per cent in the first quarter of 1990. In addition to weak foreign demand, rapidly-rising imports have depressed output. Reflecting import liberalisation the year-to-year growth in the value of imports (customs basis in US dollars) attained 35 per cent in the first three months of 1990, compared with 20 per cent for exports. However, these overall figures mask important differences between trade on a clearing and convertible-currency basis. The policy of curbing exports on a clearing basis in order to reduce the accumulated large surplus on clearing account appears to be better implemented in 1990. Exports on a clearing basis actually declined by 6 per cent year-on-year, whereas those in convertible currencies rose by 30 per cent (the corresponding import growth rates are 20 per cent and 40 per cent respectively). The trade deficit in convertible currencies reached $631 million in the first quarter, up from some $288 million a year earlier.

If monetary policy is not relaxed and the wage freeze is adhered to inflation should further moderate up to the end of June 1990, though probably settling at a higher trend rate than the postulated 1 per cent per month target. Industrial producer prices, a leading indicator of future consumer price changes, slightly declined in April. Weak domestic demand is likely to persist throughout the first half of 1990 as high real interest rates depress fixed investment. Similarly, private consumption should remain depressed, reflecting falling real incomes since February 1990. However, import liberalisation combined with the deterioration in competitiveness since mid-1989 should make for further increases in net imports so that the contraction of output is likely to be stronger than that of domestic demand. Sluggish activity and the effects of industrial restructuring point to an increase in unemployment. After the positive leads-and-lags effects wear off, the trade deficit is likely to widen even more in the second quarter of 1990. Nonetheless, the current account in convertible currencies may remain in comfortable surplus mainly thanks to higher net invisible earnings.

Developments in the second half of 1990 will, to a large extent, depend on the results of the anti-inflation programme in the first half of the year and policy continuity. Indeed, in order to foster confidence it is important for the authorities to persuade the general public that tough anti-inflation policies will be continued as long as a reasonable degree of price stability has not been firmly established. Moreover, as experience in other high-inflation countries suggests (see Annex I), in order to prevent a reversal of the disinflation process after the early phase of stabilisation, strict policies have to be maintained long enough to eradicate inflation behaviour and expectations. Restrictive monetary and fiscal policies, including commitment to a hard-currency option should, therefore, remain the two main

Diagram 11. **CONJUNCTURAL INDICATORS**
1985 = 100

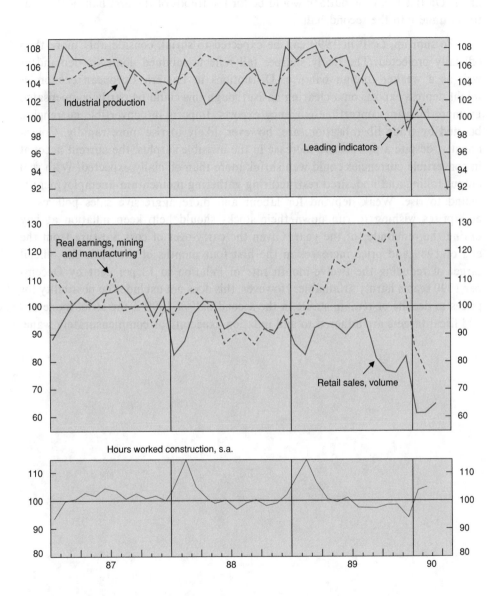

1. Yugoslav series on real earnings showing the month to which wages pertain and not when actual payments are made.

Source : OECD, *Main Economic Indicators.*

pillars of the anti-inflation programme. To the extent that this can be taken for granted, wage controls could be lifted without jeopardising earlier stabilisation gains. On this basis the outlook would be for the trends of the first half of the year to continue into the second half.

To sum up, GSP in 1990 can be expected to shrink considerably more than officially projected. The likely sharper fall reflects subdued domestic demand as well as a weaker foreign balance. Disruptions in Eastern European economies might depress exports on a clearing basis, though this could be partly compensated by more buoyant convertible-currency exports. Imports in convertible currencies, boosted by trade liberalisation, are, however, likely to rise more rapidly. Consequently, despite a prospective increase in the invisible surplus, the current account in convertible currencies could well shrink more than officially expected. With real output falling and undesired restructuring gathering momentum unemployment is bound to rise. Weak demand for labour and more aggressive sales policies of enterprises wishing to run down their stocks should help keep inflation at bay during the remainder of the year. Given the carry-over of cost pressure from the end of 1989 and price increases in the first four months of the year, the official target of reducing the twelve-month rate of inflation to 13 per cent by December 1990 seems hardly attainable. However, this does not exclude the possibility for prices to decline or remain stable in the second half of 1990 if the strict monetary and fiscal targets are adhered to and inflation expectations commensurately wane.

IV. Conclusions

Over the past two years the process of sweeping reforms aimed at establishing effective nation-wide markets for goods, labour and capital has gathered appreciable momentum. Recognising that political interference and administrative controls have stymied market-oriented developments in the past, most impediments to private initiative have now been lifted. By addressing the long-standing problems of financial indiscipline in the enterprise and banking sectors and the inefficacy of instruments of monetary control, the measures adopted should enhance economic efficiency and contribute to bringing about a lasting reduction of inflation to low rates – two prerequisites for the return of the economy to a satisfactory and sustainable growth path.

Even allowing for inevitable adjustment costs and time lags before intended results of previous reforms begin to show up, the actual performance of the economy has remained disappointing during the past two years: both aggregate output and employment were flat or declining and the rise in prices surged to rates of hyperinflation. An undeniable positive result of the IMF-supported economic programme of mid-1988 was, however, its success in averting an external liquidity crisis and in strengthening the balance of payments and the external reserve position.

Apart from inevitable delays in the implementation of such radical structural reforms and the usual problems of transition, the most important reasons behind the failure of the economy to show an early positive response to the 1988/89 liberalisation measures were the low priority assigned by the authorities to containing inflation and, related to this, the underestimation of forces capable of setting in motion a self-feeding process of runaway inflation. As suggested in the 1988 *OECD Survey of Yugoslavia*, the danger of a rebound of inflation after the ending of the price freeze in May 1988 would have justified the continuation of some form of price-wage controls and would, above all, have called for an uncompromisingly non-accommodating monetary policy stance. Instead, incomes policies were relaxed

71

and practically abandoned before the reforms designed to strengthen financial discipline were implemented or could be expected to damp excessive wage claims; and monetary conditions were not kept sufficiently tight to curb excessive credit expansion and maintain inflation-adjusted interest rates at adequate positive levels. In addition, institutional impediments and political factors continued to hinder the pursuit of coherent and co-ordinated fiscal policies.

Faced with a rapidly deteriorating situation the authorities finally decided in December 1989 to launch a comprehensive and tough anti-inflation programme, comprising price-wage controls as well as monetary and fiscal restraint measures. A novel feature of the package was the introduction of a new convertible dinar pegged to the Deutschemark at a fixed rate and guaranteed during the six months of wage stop. By freezing wages in terms of one of the hardest European currencies a solid anchor with regard to expectations for future inflation has been provided. Much will, however, depend on how closely the wage freeze is adhered to or can be enforced through clawbacks or other penalties, and on how rigorously policies of monetary and fiscal restraint continue to be pursued.

First reactions and results are encouraging. Confidence in the stability of the dinar has been boosted as witnessed by a substantial increase in foreign-exchange reserves. The monthly rate of consumer-price inflation fell from 60 per cent at the end of 1989 to 12.7 per cent in February and further to 4.0 per cent in April. The main test of success or failure will, however, come only after the ending of the current wage freeze and exchange-rate guarantee. If the decline in real earnings which occurred during the first two months of the year as a result of the pass-through of earlier cost increases does not give rise to strong compensatory claims, prices should actually start falling and, for that matter, permit some recovery of real wages.

In order to consolidate the stabilisation gains achieved during the wage freeze period some form of wage-price surveillance should be maintained. This should not rule out the lifting of wage controls and further price liberalisation after the end of the first phase of the stabilisation at the end of June 1990. Surveillance would help underline the commitment to eradicate high inflation, thereby dissuading enterprises and labour from abusing dominant market positions. This is all the more important as under self-management a smoothly functioning wage bargaining system is difficult to operate. In such a situation the role of monetary policy is even more crucial. To keep inflation and inflation expectations under tight control it is essential to restrain the expansion of liquidity and nominal demand while actively encouraging import and domestic competition. Another requirement for arresting speculative forces and combating financial laxity is to pursue a non-accommodating exchange-rate policy. In conjunction with a restrictive monetary policy stance, sticking to the hard-currency exchange rate option would reinforce policy credibility and greatly help to achieve a lasting reduction to inflation. In fact, as long as there is no major run-down of the comfortably high foreign-exchange reserves and prices at home do not tend to rise much faster than abroad, the dinar should be permitted to appreciate in real terms so as to keep a lid on domestic inflation.

The liberalisation of foreign trade and payments in conjunction with the removal of constraints to private initiatives should strengthen direct investment in Yugoslavia and help to expand the country's large unexploited export potential. The recent surge in applications for joint ventures is encouraging in this respect, though the overall sums involved are still relatively modest. As already noted in previous OECD Surveys, there are wide productivity differentials within the country as well as relative to more advanced industrialised countries, and wages of qualified labour are very low by OECD standards. The favourable development potential reflected in these differentials suggests that Yugoslavia could well become a structural net capital importer in the medium to long term. In the short term, however, Yugoslavia's current surplus and high foreign-exchange reserves are undoubtedly helpful in sustaining the credibility needed for the successful pursuit of the stabilisation programme.

The new laws concerning the organisation and operation of the socialised banking and enterprise sector call for or will prompt fundamental changes in the economic system of Yugoslavia and can therefore be expected to make the biggest contribution to strengthening market mechanisms and economic efficiency as well as to reducing the regional fragmentation of markets. However, in order to draw the full benefit in terms of new investment and innovation, it is important to remove existing or perceived ambiguities as to the definition and interpretations of ownership, property rights and management rights. The Law on Social Capital, for example, stipulates that in case of mergers or joint ventures management rights will be proportionately divided according to each partner's share in the capital stock but is rather vague on how these rights have to be shared with the workers' council. This might discourage potential foreign and domestic investors. Also, in the case of socialised or mixed enterprises it is not clear who exercises the ownership rights for the social capital which in principle belongs to all Yugoslav citizens.

In a properly-functioning market economy where capital should be induced to move to where it could yield the highest economic or social rate of return, it is clearly essential that the use of capital is not free of charge, as is the case with social capital. To counter the tendency in socialised enterprises of excessive income disbursements statutory capital accumulation rates have often been imposed but have rarely been adhered to; and, if observed, they have locked capital in companies which may not have offered the best investment opportunity. Moreover, such regulations do not solve the problem of spreading or sharing more equitably the rental income among Yugoslav citizens. The absence of a market-oriented charge or tax on the use of social capital tends to discourage socialised enterprises both from going public by selling shares and from going private by selling the entire company to a private owner. Only enterprises in trouble or in search of equity capital have an incentive to do so. The proceeds of such a surcharge on the use of capital could either go to one of the Special Agencies which are being created and will be responsible for the administration of the proceeds from asset sales by socialised enterprises, or could be used, as already suggested in the 1988 OECD Survey, for financing a development bank with a nation-wide network, extending credit on purely commercial criteria.

The imposition of new prudential criteria on commercial banks and tighter controls should also help improve the functioning of the emerging capital market and the efficiency of the banking system. However, the problem of dependence of bank managers on their clients has not been solved. By not permitting individuals to acquire voting shares of banks and not transforming banks into commercial institutions, the founding enterprises will continue to enjoy privileged access to credits. By lifting the ban on voting rights of individuals, the diffusion of shareholding of banks would be promoted so that bank managers could play their proper role and ensure the independence of banks. Similarly, problems remain with respect to the exposure of the National Bank of Yugoslavia to political leverage at the republican level. The recently-proposed substitution of the Board of Governors, as representatives of regional central banks, by a Board of Independent Experts from all republics and provinces should help ensure greater independence of the NBY from its constituent central-regional banks. Otherwise, the new National Bank Law enacted in the summer of 1989 has strengthened the position of the Governor of the Bank and has considerably improved the arsenal of monetary tools and possibilities to control money supply.

The consolidation of public sector accounts is another area where progress has been achieved more recently or will be made by the inclusion of off-budget items into the budget and the take-over of servicing costs of the NBY's foreign-exchange liabilities to banks and of selective credits. It is to be hoped that republics, provinces and municipalities are following suit in consolidating their own accounts and budgets so that a better basis is provided for fiscal co-operation and co-ordination.

Equally important is the harmonisation of taxation throughout the Federation where not much progress has as yet been made. Disparities in tax rates, tax bases and exemptions between regions, sectors and branches of industry have hampered the integration of the Yugoslav economy, with adverse effects on competition and the allocation of resources. Moreover, the heavy reliance of federal finance on customs duties and indirect taxation, and the small size of the federal budget relative to total government finance unduly restricts the scope of the central government in the pursuit of both supply-side and demand-management objectives. The recently-proposed constitutional amendments, if adopted, should help overcome long-standing problems in this area.

It is to be noted in this context that the implementation of the reform laws will not be without costs in the short run. The rehabilitation and restructuring of the enterprise and banking sector may not be accomplished within a reasonable spell of time without supporting policies and will at any rate be accompanied by higher unemployment. Active labour-market and income-support policies need to be pursued both with a view to sharing the social costs of unemployment falling upon individuals concerned and to reducing the costs for the economy as a whole by promoting labour mobility between enterprises, regions and skills. The fiscal provisions which have already been made for these purposes are welcome but after careful evaluation of short-term costs and long-run benefits they may prove to fall short of requirements.

To sum up, an impressive number of market-oriented reforms have been introduced during the last couple of years, representing a clear break with the past and triggering off moves towards political pluralism which in turn should reinforce the reform process. What is needed is patience and perseverance since the positive effects of the reforms will inevitably take time before being felt. Moreover, in certain areas, notably in the domain of federal government control and domestic competition, further efforts are called for to reduce remaining systemic weaknesses. By strengthening the role of federal institutions, better co-ordination and improved public sector efficiency could be achieved. Once the necessary reforms have been put in place it is up to the economic agents to respond positively to the new "frame conditions" and the more competitive environment. However, for this to happen a lasting reduction of inflation has to be achieved. It would therefore seem imperative not to relax the tight macroeconomic policy stance, including the maintenance of a non-accommodating exchange-rate policy. Given the resolve of the present Government to eradicate inflation and the credibility it is building up in this respect, overall conditions for better macroeconomic and microeconomic performance have rarely been so favourable. However, risks of disruptive shocks to the disinflation process have remained and have to be kept under firm control. Only if they are will it be possible to avoid a relapse of the economy into a new vicious circle of stagflation and balance-of-payments difficulties.

Notes

1. See OECD *Economic Surveys of Yugoslavia,* January 1987 and 1987/1988.

2. See OECD, *Economic Survey of Yugoslavia 1987/88*, Part IV.

3. The SDK is established on municipal, republican and federal levels and its role is firstly to control the financial operations of all socialised enterprises and public-sector agencies so that they comply with the various statutory obligations (distribution of income between profits and wages, taxes, debt repayments etc.); secondly, all these enterprises and public agencies have accounts with the SDK and all their financial transactions are made through these accounts.

4. The valuation effect results from dinar depreciations or appreciations and represents the associated automatic increase or decrease in dinar terms of the financial system's liabilities in foreign exchange to residents (mainly households).

5. Real wage statistics are difficult to establish in periods of high and accelerating inflation. A complicating factor in Yugoslavia is that the statistics on monthly wages refer to the month to which wages pertain, even if for large categories actual wage payments are made in the following month. This explains the implausible 40 per cent rise in real wages between December 1988 and November 1989 shown in the official Yugoslav statistics. The OECD Secretariat has for the purpose of this Survey adjusted the original monthly nominal wage series so that the monthly price and wage data correspond more closely.

6. Collective consumption according to Yugoslav definitions includes only material expenditure and, therefore, roughly corresponds to government consumption less the wage bill of public servants on an SNA basis.

7. Official statistics of stock levels and stock changes are not reliable, especially in periods of high inflation. The published large negative contribution of stockbuilding to GSP growth in 1989 probably exaggerates the actual drop in inventory formation as the even larger positive contribution of the statistical discrepancy is likely to reflect an important measure of unrecorded stockbuilding.

8. In Slovenia there is full employment – job-seekers represent 2.7 per cent of the active population, with little change in the ratio since the early 1980s. By contrast, job-seekers in Kosovo account for about 25.2 per cent of the active population. In Serbia, the biggest republic, the rate is about the average for Yugoslavia as a whole.

9. Reflecting growing debt-servicing charges and the need to ameliorate international competitiveness, the authorities, since the onset of the external debt crisis in the early

1980s, tried to increase the share of exports in convertible currencies and decrease that on a clearing basis. The marked reduction in the oil bill (mainly from the USSR) since the mid-1980s has favoured this shift.

10. Measured in DM, in which currency most transactions are made, emigrant remittances actually declined in 1989 and were some 40 per cent below the peak in 1985.

11. The discount averaged about 50 per cent but there were also some debt-for-equity swaps and certain banks accepted payment in goods instead of money.

12. In this context it is worth noting that the pegging of the dinar to the DM (19th December 1989) was not accompanied by an immediate alignment of interest rates on dinar deposits to the interest rate on DM deposits. As a result many people made sizeable profits by converting DMs and placing them for the rest of the month in dinar accounts with a yield of 50 per cent per month.

13. The large stock of (uncovered) foreign-exchange liabilities of the NBY to domestic banks is the result of the introduction by the Government in 1978 of a foreign-exchange insurance scheme. At that time the NBY accepted to enter in its balance sheets a foreign-exchange liability *vis-à-vis* the commercial banks against dinar claims on the banks equalling the amount of banks' (largely uncovered) foreign-exchange liabilities to private households. This operation did not generate any immediate monetary impact but proved costly for the NBY thereafter as each devaluation of the dinar raised its liabilities in dinar terms to the banks without a corresponding increase in its claims.

14. Apart from the absence of organised capital markets enterprises have had little incentive to invest in or to buy up other enterprises as this meant complete loss of control over the capital invested.

15. Yugoslavia has one of the smallest export concentration indices in the world, demonstrating the fact that Yugoslavia produces and exports a greater number of products than warranted by her size and level of development (see OECD, *Economic Survey of Yugoslavia 1987/88*, Part III).

16. In order to promote small and medium-scale enterprises, republican agencies are being set up a long with a co-ordinating agency on the federal level. The agencies will be financed by EFTA and Workd Bank Funds and by domestic private and public sources. In addition the establishment of consultancy companies is planned, with participation of domestic and foreign experts. The aim is to provide guidance both to enterprises and governments in the implementation of structural adjustment policies.

17. Self-managed enterprises would produce optimal solutions if all workers were holding life-time employment contracts, had perfect foresight and were consciously aiming at maximising their lifetime income. See Vanek J., "The general theory of labour-managed market economies", *Ithaca,* Cornell University Press, 1970.

18. Quotas effectively protect one-fifth of Yugoslav production (mainly farm products, ferrous and non-ferrous metals, metal products, chemicals, certain textiles and clothing). Computed on the basis of total imports average tariffs officially are about 7 per cent. However, tariff rates differ considerably. There are none or they are very low on raw and intermediate materials, while they are high on capital and highest on

consumer goods. In addition to tariffs, domestic taxes bring the average tax rate on total imports to almost 14 per cent (13 per cent excluding oil) on the basis of official estimates.

19. During the year ending March 1990 more than 1 200 contracts were approved.

20. The actual amount was reportedly higher, as the obligation to convert the total amount of the direct investment into dinars led most foreign companies not to declare the total value of their investment.

21. This obligation has been an important factor behind the rise in employment in the face of stagnating output during the 1980s.

22. $50 million for traditional social assistance to the lowest income households and $100 million for financing programmes for redundant labour, including retraining and job-creation schemes.

23. As evidenced by the growing proportion of household financial assets held in foreign-currency accounts a very high degree of convertibility of the dinar existed through the 1980s. However, individuals had to buy the foreign exchange on the black market at a premium.

24. The special turnover tax rate on a few services provided by foreign representatives and domestic intermediaries mainly deriving their income from commissions was fixed at 20 per cent.

25. The sizeable increases in administered prices under the package of the 18th December took place after the 20th of the month, when the price index for the month is usually finalised. The authorities decided to present a new index together with the old index which is based on data collected up to the 20th of each month. This new index covers only retail prices (not consumer prices) and only big towns and not all the country as the old one. For December the new index covers 40 days up to the 31st of the month and for subsequent months the 30 days up to the end of each month. Retail price increases on the basis of the new index (old index) are for December 64.4 (58.8) per cent, January 17.3 (41.5) per cent, February 8.4 (13.6) cent, March 2.8 (5.2) per cent and for April -0.2 (2.8) per cent.

Annex I

Yugoslav anti-inflation programme in the light of other countries' experience

In the middle of the 1980s, a number of countries at a stage of development similar to that of Yugoslavia faced a hyperinflation situation. At the end of 1984 and first months of 1985, inflation rates per month reached two-digit levels in Argentina, Bolivia and Israel, with a strong tendency to accelerate; the same occured in Brazil at the end of 1985. These trends led to the introduction of anti-inflation programmes, which are interesting to compare with the recent measures adopted in Yugoslavia.

The monetisation of large and moreover rising public-sector deficits is the common factor behind the inflation proneness in the above-mentioned countries, including Yugoslavia, where the public-sector deficit has long been disguised in the central bank accounts. As a consequence, a major task of the anti-inflation programmes is to reduce such public-sector deficits and limit money-supply growth. This largely involved a reduction of subsidies to ailing enterprises.

In order to implement such structural measures, it is crucial to break deeply-ingrained inflation expectations. To achieve this, two main instruments have been used. First, in all five countries a new currency was introduced and, except in Bolivia, pegged to a "hard" currency, which was the US dollar in Latin American countries and Israel, and the Deutschemark in the case of Yugoslavia. Secondly, wages and some or all prices were frozen, again with the exception of Bolivia. But the use of such administrative controls can only succeed in breaking inflation expectations if government policies are credible. The lack of credibility often goes hand-in-hand with a significant deterioration in the balance-of-payments position, which may lead to expectations of currency devaluation and higher inflation. One originality of the Yugoslav anti-inflation programme is that the new dinar is fully convertible, and individuals are allowed to hold foreign-exchange deposits without restrictions, which reinforces the exchange-rate guarantee for both incomes and savings. In all countries considered, the accumulation of a large stock of foreign-exchange reserves was seen as important, as indeed it is, to strengthen the credibility of the programme. Therefore, the accumulation of a large stock of foreign exchange reserves in the NBY may be an advantage for the Yugoslav programme in that respect. Finally the fact that prices have only been partly frozen in Yugoslavia may also contribute to enhance confidence.

It is interesting to note that first results of anti-inflation programmes were encouraging in all countries. Inflation typically falls to single-digit rates very quickly. However, inflation has been kept durably at bay only in Bolivia and Israel, where public-sector deficits were considerably reduced. The experience of these two countries confirms the Dornbusch and Fisher findings that real interest rates remain very high for a long period, even after inflation has been curbed[1]. Indeed, an important lesson emerging from hyperinflation experiences is that the time it takes to dampen high-inflation expectations is relatively long. For instance, in the case of Israel, monthly real interest rates, which exceeded 10 per cent during the first month of application of the programme, remained at a high 5 per cent rate

International comparison of anti-inflation programmes

	Argentina	Bolivia	Brazil	Israel	Yugoslavia
Date of the programme	Jun. 85	Aug. 85	Feb. 86	July 85	Dec. 89
Starting position					
Monthly consumer-price inflation	32	66	14	15	59
Current balance position (per cent of GNP)	-3.2[1]	-2.7[1]	-0.1[2]	-5.3[1]	+3.6[3]
Public-sector balance (per cent of GNP)	-10.1[1]	-35.6[1]	-28.1[2]	-18.9[1]	-5.0[3]
Foreign debt (per cent of GNP)	53.6[1]	123.5[1]	48.0[1]	92.5[1]	27.0[3]
Anti-inflation measures					
Exchange rate	Pegged to US $	Floating	Pegged to US $	Pegged to US $	Pegged to DM (6 months)
Wages	Frozen (6 months)	Free	Frozen	Frozen	Frozen (6 months)
Prices	Frozen	Free	Frozen	Frozen	Partially frozen
Public-sector deficit	Reduction	Reduction	No measures	Reduction	Reduction
Initial results					
Monthly consumer-price inflation					
1st month	6.2	56.5	7.8	3.9	17.3
2nd month	3.1	-2.0	1.1	3.0	8.5
3rd month	2.0	3.2	0.8	4.7	2.6
Final results					
Consumer-price inflation					
1985	672	11 750	227	305	
1986	90	276	145	48	
1987	131	15	230	20	
Public-sector balance (per cent of GNP)					
1985	-7.9	-42.6	-28.1	-5.7	
1986	-4.1	-1.2	-11.1	+0.8	
1987	-6.5	-0.2	-31.4		

1. 1984.
2. 1985.
3. 1989.
Sources : IMF, *Financial Statistics;* World Bank and OECD statistics on foreign debt.

81

(80 per cent in annual terms) nine months later. In this context, the high inflation-adjusted interest rates that currently prevail in Yugoslavia may well persist for a relatively long period, until high-inflation expectations are curbed, and should not lead to an early relaxation of monetary policy.

Another lesson to be drawn from experiences in fighting hyperinflation is that the external credibility of the programme is vital. Constant nominal exchange rates combined with positive, if small, inflation differentials erode foreign competitiveness with detrimental consequences for the external balances. Even in Argentina and Brazil, but also in the case of Israel in early 1980s, commendable efforts were made to reduce public deficits and tighten monetary conditions, but the programmes failed because the deterioration in the balance of payments fuelled expectations of currency devaluations which were "validated" by later adjustments to the exchange rate. By contrast, with the 1985 programme, Israel received external support which alleviated the balance of payments problem. In the case of Bolivia, the tough macro-policy stance led to a recession, thus offsetting the detrimental effects on the external accounts coming from the real exchange rate appreciation. The Bolivian recession was however mild and of very short duration. Moreover, as noted in other studies[2], over the medium term output growth in countries that have succeeded in suppressing hyperinflation has not been less than in countries where anti-inflation measures failed.

The main conclusion which could perhaps be drawn from the other countries' experience in fighting hyperinflation is that success of an anti-inflation programme crucially depends upon two factors: the tenacity of the government to adhere to its policy objectives, even at the cost of a recession, and the maintainance of a sound balance of payments position so as to assure the credibility ot the programme.

Notes

1. See Dornbusch, R. and Fisher, S., "Stopping Hyperinflations Past and Present", NBER working paper, December 1985.
2. See Blejer, M. and Liviatan, N., "Fighting Hyperinflation: Stabilisation Strategies in Argentina and Israel, 1985-86", IMF Staff Papers, 34(3), September 1987, and references therein.

Calendar of main economic events

1988

April

End of the partial price and wage freeze introduced in November 1987.

May

In conjunction with anti-inflation measures, important deregulation policies were introduced, for the first time, on 15th May:

- Imposition of ceilings on wage increases: the year-on-year growth in the first half of 1988 limited to 139 per cent, in the first nine months to 132 per cent and in 1988 as a whole to 119 per cent;
- Public expenditure, except pensions, targeted to rise 10 per cent less than expected inflation;
- The 1988 growth target for net dinar assets of the banking system (excluding valuation effect) fixed at 26 per cent and that for net dinar assets of NBY to 15 per cent. Inflation-adjusted interest rates to become positive;
- Extensive price liberalisation initiated with the share of freely formed producer prices for goods set to increase to 60 per cent in May and to 70 per cent by December;
- Abolition of administrative controls over the allocation of foreign exchange and the establishment of a unified foreign exchange market, where the exchange rate would be determined by demand and supply;
- Extensive import liberalisation. The share of free imports raised from 14 to 40 per cent of total imports (planned to 50 per cent by the end of 1988) and that of imports under quotas and licenses reduced from 51 per cent to 26 per cent.

June

The NBY discount rate to be raised to the level of retail-price inflation.

October

Wage controls abolished.

The new law on social accounting introduces inflation accounting instead of historic cost accounting, so as to oblige enterprises to revalue assets.

Interest-rate policy measures: inflation-adjusted interest rate on deposits fixed at 5 per cent; public sector surpluses deposited with banks no longer remunerated; short-term interest rates on foreign exchange deposits to be increased so that their level is 2 percentage points above that of similar deposits abroad (4 points for deposits with a maturity of one-year or more); the discount rate of NBY to be determined monthly using the retail-price increase of the previous month as a minimum (for October it was fixed at 13.89 per cent compared with 15.69 per cent in September); interest rate on selective credits decreased from 65 to 50 per cent of the discount rate.

December

Law on enterprises and law on foreign investment introduces private ownership and mixed ownership. The law on enterprises distinguishes four types of enterprises: "socially-owned", "co-operatives", "private" (owned by individuals, including foreigners, or civil legal entities) and "mixed" (i.e. involving assets owned by two or more of the following: socially-owned enterprises, co-operatives and private). Any of the above can take the form of a "joint-stock" company, a "limited liability" company, a "limited partnership" company or a company with "unlimited joint and several liability". Enterprises employing less than 100 workers are considered as "small-scale businesses".

The official real and nominal targets for 1989 are: GSP 1.5 per cent, industrial output 1 per cent, agricultural production 6 per cent, volume exports and imports of goods and services 5 per cent and 8.3 per cent respectively and a convertible balance of payments surplus of $1 435 million.

Creation of the Yugoslav Bank for International Co-operation for financing and insuring exports.

Resignation of the federal government of Mrs. Mikulic, but remaining in office as a caretaker government.

The 1989 growth target for net dinar credits (excluding valuation effects) is fixed at 32.4 per cent.

1989

January

Revenue of government agencies proper (socio-political communities) is budgeted to increase by 10 per cent less than retail-price inflation and revenue of social agencies (self-management communities of interest) by 5 per cent less.

Further liberalisation of prices and imports. Abolition of certain import taxes.

February

Between 11th February and the 10th April obligatory reserves on deposits to be raised from 14 to 15 per cent.

The proportion of selective-credits rediscounted by the NBY is cut by 20 per cent.

The law on banks and other financial organisations passed by the Federal Assembly.

March

New mechanism of obligatory bank reserves introduced: for sight deposits and short-term time deposits the obligatory deposit rate is 21 per cent, for time deposits over three months 5 per cent and on deposits for house building 2 per cent. At the same time the interest rate on obligatory deposits paid by NBY increased from 15 to 25 per cent.

Formation of a new federal government (15th March), with Mr. Markovic as Prime Minister.

Additional price liberalisation measures introduced.

Further import liberalisation, so that more than two-thirds of capital goods' imports freed. In addition, most impediments on imports by private sector firms abolished.

Abolition of the ceilings on amounts that private persons can withdraw in cash from their foreign exchange accounts.

A new law passed on the National Bank of Yugoslavia and on the Uniform Monetary Operations of the National Banks of the Republics and the Autonomous Provinces.

April

Henceforth, the discount rate to be fixed monthly and be based on the forecast inflation for the month, to which a margin is added so as to achieve a positive real rate.

May

New Laws amending and supplementing the Law on Banks and Other Financial Organisations as well as the Law on Enterprises.

Enterprises' promissory notes fully guaranteed by banks reduced from 40 per cent to 20 per cent of short-term bank assets.

June

Reflecting the overshooting of initial targets the new target for net domestic assets fixed at 645 per cent (including valuation effects) for 1989.

Measures aimed at reducing trade with eastern European countries, including restrictions on import payments, tighter controls on volume of trade and changing payment contracts with the USSR.

July

Consolidation of budget and extra-budget accounts at the federal level and reduction of expenditures for economic intervention.

Amendments to Accounting law reducing the obligatory full revaluation of assets to only 60 per cent of items.

Promissory notes guaranteed by banks to be abolished as from September 1989.

Further import liberalisation so that 77 per cent of imports are no longer subject to restrictions.

August

Measures for stimulating agricultural production, including an increase in the credit rediscounted for financing agricultural activities, and, for the first time, the possibility for private farmers to obtain selective credits.

Government ruling with the aim of forcing enterprises to increase transparency for price formation, so that all cost elements are clearly shown.

September

The growth of wages to be linked to financial results from previous accounting period as from 1st October. Wage increases pertaining to August and September limited to 90 per cent of the increase in cost of living.

Further liberalisation of prices. The share of products whose prices require approval by Federal bureau for prices reduced from 2.2 to 0.7 per cent of total products, products under the cost-linked automatic increase category reduced from 13.4 to 13 per cent and the proportion of freely determined prices increased to 74 per cent.

October

Elimination of the indirect price control mechanisms ("on common elements" and "cost-linked automatic increases") and restoration of direct control by the Federal government on 23.2 per cent of producer prices. At the same time the percentage of freely formed producer prices raised to 75.1 per cent.

Abolition of full indexation for the rate of interest and exchange rate. The monthly rate of interest and devaluation of the dinar set at 30 per cent compared with a rate of inflation of almost 50 per cent in September.

November

The proportion of administered prices raised to 24.3 per cent at the end of November.

Social compact aiming at decreasing the share of public consumption in GSP in 1990. Revenues of government agencies proper to rise 5 per cent less and revenues of social agencies 2 per cent less than retail prices.

December

Adoption of an anti-inflation programme, including the introduction of the new dinar (equal to 10 000 old dinars), convertible and pegged to the Deutschemark at an exchange rate of 1 DM for 7 new dinars and a wage freeze and a partial price freeze for a period of six months.

Obligation to finance the federal expenditure by increasing taxation and to a smaller extent by issuing government paper. Resort to NBY credits to be discontinued.

Growth targets for net dinar assets of banking system for 1990 fixed at 7 per cent and for M1 at 24 per cent.

New laws: on "social capital", on "rehabilitation, bankruptcy and liquidation of enterprises", on "forming and financing the agency for rehabilitation of banking system", on "financing social programmes", on "basic principles of taxation system" and amendments to the foreign operations law.

Federal Executive Council proposes three constitutional amendments to the Federal Assembly: firstly, with the aim of introducing pluralism of ownership and equality in treatment of different kinds of ownership, and abolition of ceilings to private land holdings. Secondly, with the aim of unifying the tax system and strengthening the role and responsibility of the Federal Government in the area of fiscal policy. Thirdly, with the aim of increasing the powers of the Governor of NBY and the responsibility of the NBY over monetary policy. In the same amendment it is proposed that the Federal Budget be no longer financed from Republican contributions and instead more taxes be raised on the federal level.

1990

January

Further constitutional amendments proposed mainly concerning public ownership, natural resources and increasing flexibility for the establishment of self-managed communities of interest.

The rate of compulsory reserves of commercial banks reduced.

February

Additional monetary measures introduced by NBY in order to neutralise the impact on money supply of the big increase in foreign exchange reserves (around $1 billion): outstanding dinar credits by commercial banks to be reduced in February to 80 per cent of the end-December level, primary money issue to be reduced by 30 per cent, commercial banks to invest 700 million dinars in NBY certificates with an interest rate 40 per cent below the NBY's discount rate, commercial banks' cash holdings to be increased by $50 million to $1 billion, interest rate on banks' compulsory reserves with the NBY raised from 12 to 25 per cent.

In order to further reduce the trade surplus with the clearing area and to stop speculative selling of foreign currency by domestic citizens to eastern European tourists the Federal Government introduced the following measures: the exchange rate for check and credit letter transactions by foreign citizens fixed at 10 per cent of the official exchange rate of the "clearing" dollar, eastern European tourists have to declare the amount of cash which they bring in and out of Yugoslavia, import of articles for sale (on black market) strictly forbidden.

For enterprises in agro-industry and for those engaged in external trade part of short-term selective credits to be converted into long-term credits (the total amount involved at the end of 1989 was 4 645 million dinars, of which 3 986 million dinars concerned enterprises in agro-industry).

In order to stop the increase in real wages through extension of fringe benefits, all payments in kind frozen and be brought back to the November 1989 level.

Introduction of subsidies for merchandise exports 7 per cent and for services 3 per cent.

IMF announced a new stand-by eighteen month agreement involving financial support amounting to $600 million.

April

Multi-party elections in the Republics of Slovenia and Croatia.

STATISTICAL ANNEX

Table A. **Social product** (Yugoslav definitions and concepts)
Millions of dinars

	1979	1980	1981	1982	1983	1984	1985	1986	1987	1988
						Current prices				
Consumers' expenditure	622 447	818 829	1 143 300	1 510 662	2 087 788	3 207 200	5 659 400	11 205 900	24 796 500	74 563 000
Collective consumption	110 900	143 060	198 200	260 140	345 119	524 300	970 000	1 910 000	4 150 000	12 970 000
Gross fixed capital formation	447 581	545 665	684 961	854 816	1 029 539	1 458 438	2 608 800	5 047 000	9 914 600	27 192 800
Change in stocks	90 940	185 546	297 705	372 602	630 959	1 232 926	2 092 800	3 948 900	9 636 500	31 536 900
Foreign balance	-128 459	-153 290	-123 395	-144 034	-98 964	-159 869	-136 300	-167 100	-688 800	-1 417 000
Exports of goods and services[1]	200 735	369 232	446 465	599 956	851 298	1 703 769	2 637 500	3 762 700	12 348 600	46 644 000
Imports of goods and services[1]	329 194	522 522	569 360	743 990	950 262	1 863 638	2 773 800	3 929 800	13 037 400	48 061 000
Statistical discrepancy	22 008	13 279	7 479	70 648	69 848	62 848	90 000	110 000	1 455 900	3 715 000
Social product	1 165 417	1 553 089	2 208 250	2 924 834	4 064 289	6 325 843	11 284 700	22054 700	49 264 700	148 560 700
						1972 prices				
Consumers' expenditure	197 101	198 481	196 496	196 345	192 919	190 990	190 900	199 400	200 100	197 400
Collective consumption	34 015	33 670	32 050	31 820	30 194	30 125	30 700	32 110	31 600	31 700
Gross fixed capital formation	128 293	120 717	108 887	102 892	92 900	83 979	80 903	83 706	79 400	74 800
Change in stocks	29 054	45 499	52 092	49 450	59 654	76 346	80 170	80 250	..	..
Foreign balance	-37 851	-24 670	-13 999	-13 213	-4 003	3 471	7 112	27	..	..
Exports of goods and services	70 837	76 148	85 279	69 505	66 439	70 739	76 398	74 717	..	..
Imports of goods and services	108 688	100 818	99 278	82 718	70 442	67 268	69 286	74 690	..	..
Statistical discrepancy	21 705	6 987	10 871	21 747	12 601	6 925	3 957	12 255	..	..
Social product	372 317	380 684	386 397	389 041	384 265	391 836	393 742	407 748	403 100	396 300

1. At statistical exchange rates before 1987. From 1987 onwards, at current exchange rates.
Source: Direct communication to the OECD.

Table B. **National product and expenditure** (standardized definitions and concepts)

Millions of dinars, current prices

	1979	1980	1981	1982	1983	1984	1985	1986	1987	1988[1]
Consumers' expenditure on goods and services	672 125	881 140	1 226 437	1 623 803	2 242 940	3 389 150	5 950 700	11 782 386	26 440 900	79 251 700
Government current expenditure on goods and services	227 500	290 967	380 850	499 580	642 950	931 560	1 665 900	3 347 818	7 517 800	22 520 000
Gross fixed capital formation	447 581	545 665	684 961	854 816	1 029 530	1 458 400	2 608 800	5 047 000	9 914 600	27 192 800
Change in stocks	90 940	185 546	297 705	372 602	630 959	1 232 526	2 092 800	3 948 900	9 636 500	31 536 900
Exports of goods and services[2]	200 735	369 232	446 465	599 956	851 298	1 703 769	2 637 497	3 762 675	12 348 600	46 644 000
less: Imports of goods and services[2]	329 194	522 522	569 860	743 990	950 262	1 863 638	2 773 801	3 929 858	13 037 400	48 061 000
Statistical discrepancy	-15 751	-26 330	-56 313	-48 059	-164 550	-198 305	-230 596	-559 121	-481 300	-756 100
Gross domestic product at market prices	1 293 936	1 723 698	2 410 245	3 158 708	4 282 865	6 653 462	11 951 300	23 399 800	52 339 700	158 328 300
Income from the rest of the world[2]	75 259	126 863	161 807	212 219	228 621	462 258	654 221	918 183	3 438 100	13 267 500
Income payment to the rest of the world[2]	16 359	36 118	58 886	87 947	112 281	239 492	363 229	497 845	1 474 400	5 425 500
Gross national product at market prices	1 352 836	1 814 443	2 513 166	3 282 980	4 399 205	6 876 228	12 242 292	23 820 138	54 303 400	166 170 300
Indirect taxes	163 085	195 332	269 014	339 970	508 213	771 134	1 192 950	2 363 749	5 147 600	15 657 100
Subsidies	34 233	42 894	50 711	79 430	108 893	171 742	316 469	616 830	1 524 100	3 779 200
Gross national product at factor cost	1 223 984	1 662 005	2 294 863	3 022 440	3 999 885	6 276 836	11 365 811	22 073 219	50 679 900	154 292 400
Depreciation and funds for other purposes	128 507	174 746	236 125	374 535	529 490	779 347	1 325 400	2 491 800	6 662 800	19 299 100
Net national product at factor cost	1 095 477	1 487 259	2 058 738	2 647 905	3 470 395	5 497 489	10 040 411	19 581 419	44 017 100	134 993 300

1. Preliminary data.
2. At statistical exchange rates before 1987. From 1987 onwards, at current exchange rates.
Source: Direct communication to the OECD.

91

Table C. **Gross product at factor cost by industry**

Millions of dinars, current prices

	1979	1980	1981	1982	1983	1984	1985	1986	1987	1988[1]
Agriculture, forestry and fishing	146 842	201 025	304 192	435 433	620 108	896 050	1 375 569	2 899 100	5 679 300	16 435 900
Mining and quarrying	24 315	38 544	56 919	77 204	103 807	199 820	335 579	513 820	1 364 200	3 928 800
Manufacturing	343 933	481 113	699 372	917 860	1 264 434	2 064 800	4 125 352	7 620 955	18 194 800	58 951 100
Electricity, gas and water	31 533	45 030	59 839	79 156	91 450	144 850	263 840	564 588	1 239 400	3 257 700
Construction	128 446	167 770	226 019	271 590	322 193	446 900	819 688	1 588 854	3 466 800	9 110 700
Transports and communication	97 013	127 239	176 500	227 570	309 906	469 100	890 146	1 735 021	5 509 900	16 276 200
Wholesale and retail trade	145 390	195 237	264 400	358 622	503 377	774 200	1 305 479	2 610 290	3 745 800	11 188 700
Banking, insurance, real estate and business and financial services	43 932	59 881	80 242	107 906	134 395	220 150	420 454	889 945	2 426 700	7 602 500
Community, social and personal services	203 680	255 421	324 459	422 827	533 875	838 200	1 538 712	3 230 308	7 089 300	19 698 800
Gross domestic product at factor cost	1 165 084	1 571 260	2 191 942	2 898 168	3 883 545	6 054 070	11 074 819	21 652 881	48 716 200	146 450 400
Net payment of income payable to factors of production by the rest of the world[2]	58 900	90 745	102 921	124 272	116 340	222 766	290 992	420 338	1 963 700	784 200
Gross national product at factor cost	1 223 984	1 662 005	2 294 863	3 022 440	3 999 885	6 276 836	11 365 811	22 073 219	50 679 900	154 292 400

1. Preliminary data.
2. At statistical exchange rates until 1986. From 1987 onwards, at current exchange rates.
Source: Direct communication to the OECD.

92

Table D. Gross fixed investment
Millions of dinars, current prices

	1979	1980	1981	1982	1983	1984	1985	1986	1987	1988
Total	447 600	545 600	685 000	854 800	1 029 500	1 458 400	2 608 800	5 047 000	9 914 600	27 192 800
Private sector	71 000	88 500	121 600	166 100	209 800	292 400	466 800	950 900	1 890 000	6 923 900
Social sector	376 600	457 100	563 400	688 700	819 700	1 166 000	2 142 000	4 096 100	8 024 600	20 268 900
By activity:										
Productive	319 600	386 300	485 700	603 000	740 100	1 049 500	1 929 800	3 653 800	7 364 100	18 743 100
Non-productive	128 000	159 300	199 300	251 800	289 400	408 900	679 000	1 393 200	2 550 500	8 449 700
By industry:										
Agriculture and forestry	31 500	36 700	51 200	81 800	106 200	145 500	231 500	411 600	785 700	2 224 000
Industry	157 800	199 600	254 600	305 700	376 300	540 500	998 500	1 889 700	3 999 100	9 320 500
Building	13 800	14 400	19 300	19 900	22 700	29 400	71 600	121 100	184 800	581 400
Transportation	65 900	72 900	81 200	94 100	124 600	160 800	309 900	551 500	987 300	2 948 700
Trade, catering, tourism	28 890	32 200	40 500	49 600	49 600	72 200	133 000	317 600	619 200	1 531 700
Housing, communal activities	103 600	134 200	172 500	231 200	268 000	368 500	576 500	1 174 100	2 205 300	7 381 000
Other social sector	46 110	55 600	65 700	72 500	82 100	141 500	287 500	581 400	1 133 200	3 205 500
By sector of assets:										
Machines and equipment	167 900	191 600	232 800	296 000	378 600	584 500	1 165 300	2 212 100	4 254 700	11 466 300
Domestic	109 000	125 500	163 700	206 000	266 000	407 600	784 100	1 575 100	2 954 400	8 290 400
Imported	58 900	66 100	69 100	90 000	112 600	176 900	381 200	637 000	1 300 300	3 175 900
Building	249 800	309 400	386 700	479 800	538 600	744 300	1 259 400	2 531 400	4 784 000	13 912 900
Other	29 900	44 600	65 500	79 000	112 300	129 600	184 100	303 500	875 900	1 813 600

Note: Figures include expenditures for already existing assets and indicate realised investments independent of the date of payment.
Source: Direct communication to the OECD.

Table E. National income and the household account (Yugoslav definitions and concepts)

Millions of dinars

	1980	1981	1982	1983	1984	1985	1986	1987	1988
National income									
Net wages and salaries of employees in productive enterprises and production of individual producers for own consumption	595 765	878 339	1 154 857	1 558 785	2 273 554	4 014 300	8 334 200	17 616 400	49 867 600
Tax on income and Social Security payments	260 005	349 405	454 694	616 306	958 200	1 823 900	4 190 200	10 038 300	29 405 700
Interest and enterprises taxes	306 652	429 382	574 917	887 762	1 440 200	2 757 900	5 559 500	12 250 800	48 996 600
Accumulation of productive enterprises and individual producers	238 143	346 763	411 303	536 180	965 346	1 524 500	1 825 900	3 718 900	4 378 400
National income	1 400 565	2 003 889	2 595 771	3 599 033	5 637 300	10 120 600	19 909 800	43 624 400	132 648 300
plus: Depreciation	152 524	204 361	329 023	465 256	688 500	1 164 100	2 144 900	5 640 300	15 912 400
Social product	1 553 089	2 208 250	2 924 794	4 064 289	6 325 800	11 284 700	22 054 700	49 264 700	148 560 700
Household account									
Net wages and salaries of employees in productive enterprises and production of individual producers for own consumption	595 765	878 339	1 154 857	1 558 785	2 273 554	4 014 300	8 334 200	17 616 400	49 867 600
Net wages and salaries of employees in non-productive enterprises	150 507	191 314	247 609	318 109	459 986	828 600	1 723 800	3 803 700	10 990 800
Receipts from Social Security and other welfare funds	158 549	209 138	284 523	377 101	534 599	961 300	2 278 200	5 338 700	14 896 900
Bank interest (net)	21 883	29 292	43 458	85 819	164 369	458 700	831 600	1 821 900	7 820 200
Other domestic transfer receipts	5 632	3 708	67 564	409 205	520 044	1 431 000	2 499 900	9 305 300	41 135 300
Net transfers from abroad	120 475	149 768	198 968	213 785	427 848	600 900	860 500	3 271 600	12 601 700
Total income received	1 052 811	1 461 559	1 996 979	2 962 804	4 380 400	8 294 800	16 528 200	41 157 600	137 312 500
Consumer's expenditure on goods and services of productive sector	753 590	1 045 441	1 377 769	1 889 278	2 917 200	5 171 200	10 320 200	22 901 900	68 770 300
Consumption of self-produced commodities	65 239	97 859	132 893	198 510	286 002	488 200	885 700	1 894 600	5 792 700
Consumer payment to non productive sector	82 152	105 767	140 435	190 484	283 529	470 800	920 900	2 142 300	6 148 800
Savings	151 830	212 492	345 882	684 532	893 669	2 164 600	4 401 400	14 218 800	56 600 700
Saving ratio (in %)	14.4	14.5	17.3	23.1	20.5	26.1	26.6	34.5	41.2

Source: FSO, Statisticki Godisnjak.

Table F. Agriculture

	Unit or base	1976	1977	1978	1979	1980	1981	1982	1983	1984	1985	1986	1987	1988
Indices of agricultural output	1951-1955=100													
Total		217	227	213	225	225	228	244	240	244	226	252	239	226
Crop production		205	212	186	205	204	206	227	221	225	204	235	209	196
Livestock production		244	263	268	270	273	279	293	284	293	283	289	292	280
Production of selected commodities														
Wheat	Mill. metric tons	6	5.6	5.4	4.5	5.1	4.3	5.2	5.5	5.6	4.8	4.8	5.3	6.3
Maize	–	9.1	9.9	7.6	10.1	9.3	9.8	11.1	10.7	11.3	9.9	12.5	8.9	7.7
Sugar beet	–	4.7	5.3	5.2	5.9	5.2	6.2	5.7	5.7	6.8	6.3	5.6	6.2	4.6
Meat[1]	Thous. metric tons	1 034	1 144	1 237	1 227	1 207	1 221	1 244	1 280	1 369	1 292	1 285	1 331	1 316
Forestry cuttings	Mill. cubic metres	18.5	19.5	19.7	19.9	19.4	20.4	21.1	21.3	22.6	22.4	22.8	22.3	22.1
Number of tractors in use[2]	Thousand	260.9	296.8	342	385.1	415.7	595.5	622.4	705.8	808.5	881.7	955.3	1 017	1 066
Consumption of fertilizers	Thous. metric tons	1 970	2 056	2 147	2 203	2 131	2 384	2 510	2 460	2 556	2 551	2 643	2 607	2 557

1. Production of meat in the country (exclusive of livestock for slaughter).
2. At the end of year.
Source: Direct communication to the OECD

Table G. Industrial production

	Unit or base	1977	1978	1979	1980	1981	1982	1983	1984	1985	1986	1987	1988
Indices of industrial production													
	1970=100												
Total	Original base	167	181	195	204	212	212	215	227	233	242	243	242
Mining	1985=100	139	143	148	153	158	162	164	168	177	179	181	180
Manufacturing		168	184	200	208	218	217	219	231	237	244	245	243
Basic metals		171	188	196	199	214	211	223	240	252	255	247	254
Metal products		175	199	219	226	237	238	235	245	256	265	259	256
Chemicals		206	234	251	275	301	299	327	301	309	329	341	351
Textiles		152	158	172	182	189	187	189	201	208	221	231	228
Food, drinks, tobacco		160	173	187	189	195	199	199	207	203	208	213	204
Output of selected commodities													
Electricity	Billions kWh	48.6	51.3	55.0	59.4	60.4	62.1	67.6	73.0	74.4	77.9	80.8	83.7
Lignite and brown coal	Mill. metric tons	38.6	39.2	41.7	46.6	51.5	54.2	59.0	64.7	69.1	69.5	71.8	72.6
Petroleum products[1]	–	13.8	14.2	15.8	15.2	13.4	13.6	13.4	13.9	13.1	15.1	15.3	16.3
Copper ore	–	17.5	17.1	16.4	19.6	18.3	19.7	23.4	25.3	26.2	27.9	27.7	30.1
Lead ore	Thous. metric tons	130	124	130	121	119	113	114	114	115	117	107	103
Zinc ore		112	104	102	95	89	70	87	86	89	95	87	91
Crude steel	Mill. metric tons	3.2	3.5	3.5	3.6	4.0	3.9	4.1	4.2	4.4	4.5	4.4	4.5
Cement	–	8.0	8.7	9.1	9.3	9.8	9.7	9.6	9.3	9.0	9.1	9.0	8.8
Metal and wood–working machines	Thous. metric tons	28.6	31.9	37.5	46.4	46.3	49.3	50.3	42.4	42.5	49.1	53.7	55.0
Building machines	–	47.1	67.8	82.6	71.4	71.3	63.3	48.0	80.7	92.7	99.8	87.7	41.8
Rotating machines	–	34.9	40.6	44.1	43.6	47.3	49.2	42.8	49.1	58.6	57.3	56.9	52.8
Pulp and cellulose	–	584	612	608	606	642	659	681	715	707	713	660	711
Cotton fabrics	Mill. sq. meters	384	410	418	385	377	372	379	318	344	358	366	351

1. Crude petroleum and refined.
Source: Direct communication to the OECD.

Table H. Labour force and employment
Thousands

	1977	1978	1979	1980	1981	1982	1983	1984	1985	1986	1987	1988
Active population (mid-year estimate)[1]	9 466	9 565	9 666	9 768	9 870	9 974	10 079	10 270	10 398	..	..	..
Paid employment	5 148	5 383	5 615	5 798	5 966	6 105	6 223	6 355	6 516	6 716	6 866	6 884
Registered unemployment	700	735	762	785	809	862	910	975	1 040	1 087	1 081	1 132
Other labour force[1]	3 618	3 447	3 289	3 185	3 095	3 007	2 046	2 940	2 842	..	..	..
Worker emigration (net)[2]	825	800	790	770	770	760	740	780	710	768	770	775
Yugoslav workers employed in Germany[2]	375	360	360	350	336	320	310	320	350	320	292	295
Paid domestic employment by sector:												
Social sector	5 052	5 280	5 506	5 681	5 846	5 980	6 097	6 224	6 378	6 566	6 703	6 715
Productive activities	4 182	4 364	4 560	4 709	4 848	4 955	5 052	5 162	5 294	5 452	5 559	5 556
Non-productive activities	870	916	946	972	998	1 025	1 045	1 062	1 084	1 114	1 144	1 159
Private sector (excluding agriculture)	96	103	109	117	120	125	126	131	138	150	163	169
Paid domestic employment by industry:												
Agriculture	179	183	188	191	200	210	218	226	231	239	244	245
Industry	1 954	2 022	2 102	2 162	2 242	2 313	2 374	2 445	2 529	2 625	2 706	2 716
Construction	531	567	602	622	622	612	599	592	583	586	583	554
Transportation and communication	372	381	387	399	408	416	422	480	440	452	451	477
Trade	507	529	558	582	596	607	621	631	641	656	666	671

1. Including Yugoslav workers temporarily employed abroad.
2. According to the Federal Bureau of Employment, estimates.
Source: Direct communication to the OECD.

Table I. **Prices and wages**

Indices, 1969=100

	1978	1979	1980	1981	1982	1983	1984	1985	1986	1987	1988	1989
Agricultural producer prices	417	524	709	1 087	1 471	2 174	3 137	5 019	9 091	18 454	56 100	654 687[1]
Industrial producer prices	315	357	455	658	820	1 082	1 704	3 076	5 331	10 484	31 767	414 877
Materials	354	410	550	793	1 009	1 352	2 186	4 056	6 392	11 950	37 344	494 688
Capital goods	250	265	297	372	430	524	744	1 339	2 432	4 968	13 076	194 963
Consumer goods	291	323	391	562	701	921	1 412	2 442	4 554	9 673	28 448	438 668
Export unit values, in dollars	266	305	364	395	424	423	696	741	741	752	817	..
Import unit values, in dollars	267	319	381	421	430	430	562	587	537	538	600	..
Cost of living	394	474	617	870	1 149	1 613	2 500	4 287	8 107	17 860	52 687	712 328
of which:												
Food	425	503	661	946	1 309	1 907	2 831	4 860	9 067	19 173	57 902	784 572
Services	338	407	490	623	762	1 000	1 398	2 438	4 754	11 319	33 278	428 620
Wage per person employed in social sector	513	617	744	995	1 267	1 602	2 304	4 107	8 553	17 619	47 924	808 478

1. Estimation.
Source: Direct communication to the OECD.

Table J. Consolidated balance sheet of all banks[1] excluding financial and other organisations and internal banks

Billions of dinars, end of period

	1980	1981	1982	1983	1984	1985	1986	1987	1988
Total short-term operations	860.3	1 343.5	1 967.8	3 569.9	5 927.5	10 535.2	19 129.1	75 273.6	161 416.6
Gold and foreign exchange	75.7	133.1	134.2	292.8	615.0	1 029.6	1 273.1	2 517.7	20 490.3
Foreign exchange receivables	51.2	147.2	284.9	520.8	868.0	1 157.9	2 055.0	5 387.0	22 299.4
Loans to organisations of associated labour performing economic activities	310.8	478.6	618.5	841.2	1 228.2	1 956.4	3 734.3	8 529.4	27 352.6
Loans to the Federal government and to other public institutions	3.5	2.5	2.0	1.6	1.0	1.5	8.0	55.9	24.9
Loans to households	7.6	11.8	10.9	11.1	14.6	23.2	54.8	104.5	307.8
Other assets[2]	411.5	570.3	917.3	1 902.4	3 200.7	6 366.6	12 003.9	58 679.1	90 941.6
Total long-term operations	1 187.1	1 393.4	1 723.3	2 325.0	3 432.6	5 109.0	8 274.8	18 302.3	65 833.3
Foreign exchange receivables from the rest of the world	20.7	25.8	32.2	48.1	69.9	108.6	157.5	357.0	3 906.3
Loans to organisations of associated labour performing economic activities	802.0	896.7	1 108.4	1 617.2	2 511.5	3 729.5	6 218.6	1 5131.6	56 015.6
Loans to the Federal government and to other public institutions	34.3	39.8	41.3	42.2	48.5	65.8	76.8	80.5	120.0
Loans to households	57.3	63.3	91.6	106.3	171.7	251.2	247.0	210.2	275.4
Loans for housing construction	91.8	132.7	170.7	189.9	228.8	312.5	576.0	666.6	1 079.3
Other assets[3]	181.0	235.1	279.1	321.3	402.2	641.4	998.9	1 856.4	4 436.7
Funds	27.4	31.9	40.3	51.2	70.9	112.2	234.8	732.9	2 270.2
Total assets	2 074.8	2 768.8	3 731.4	5 946.1	9 431.0	15 756.4	27 638.7	94 308.8	229 520.1
Total short-term liabilities	1 258.5	1 683.1	2 249.3	3 363.1	5 305.8	8 900.9	15 941.6	64 012.2	115 288.3
Foreign exchange liabilities	321.5	477.3	646.4	1 152.7	1 816.8	2 580.7	4 128.3	11 236.3	41 447.5
Money supply	461.6	584.3	739.7	888.7	1 272.0	1 863.5	3 895.9	7 786.1	25 193.5
Other and restricted deposits	253.6	328.8	507.5	630.0	1 063.7	1 827.1	3 126.8	5 020.9	14 426.7
Other[4]	221.8	292.7	355.7	691.7	1 153.3	2 629.6	4 790.6	39 968.9	34 220.6
Total long-term operations	769.7	998.9	1 377.5	2 457.5	3 961.6	6 611.6	11 146.2	29 228.4	111 213.5
Foreign exchange liabilities	349.6	512.1	783.7	1 715.7	2 961.8	5 083.7	8 544.2	25 112.3	100 487.9
Time deposits	163.1	208.4	252.1	298.3	459.3	708.2	1 350.7	2 201.5	5 621.1
Loans	257.0	278.4	341.7	443.5	540.5	819.7	1 251.3	1 914.6	5 104.5
Funds	74.0	86.7	104.6	125.5	163.6	243.9	490.8	1 068.1	3 018.4
Total liabilities	2 102.2	2 768.7	3 731.4	5 946.1	9 431.0	15 756.4	27 578.6	94 308.7	229 520.2

1. Data have been recalculated in line with a new methodology of the National Bank of Yugoslavia.
2. Placements in securities and other receivables.
3. Placements in securities, share in international financial organisations and other receivables.
4. Issued securities, receivables in payment operations and other liabilities.
Source: National bank of Yugoslavia.

Table K. Imports and exports by commodity groups[1]

Millions of US dollars

SITC SECTIONS	1976	1977	1978	1979	1980	1981	1982	1983	1984	1985	1986	1987	1988
Imports													
0. and 1. Food, drink and tobacco	637	784	605	977	991	788	689	594	423	385	757	729	787
of which: Cereals and cereal preparations	142	92	20	271	302	98	228	68	61	27	82	18	43
2. Raw materials	693	940	995	1 205	1 544	1 637	1 422	1 313	1 423	1 458	1 235	1 160	1 435
of which: Textile fibres and waste	248	335	348	376	415	457	424	324	439	452	372	287	356
3. Mineral fuels	1 082	1 296	1 431	2 248	3 549	3 786	3 433	3 304	3 515	3 307	2 606	2 195	2 385
5. Chemicals	791	989	1 140	1 653	1 824	2 027	1 658	1 758	1 756	1 665	1 590	2 055	2 291
6. Semi-manufactures	1 364	1 763	1 698	2 243	2 376	2 595	2 007	1 845	1 822	1 951	1 829	2 092	2 048
of which: Base metals	700	841	835	1 151	1 313	1 419	1 040	903	320	1 031	904	881	607
7. and 8. Finished manufactures	2 731	3 791	4 058	5 637	4 674	4 816	4 071	3 243	2 956	3 290	3 666	4 350	4 181
of which: Machinery	1 935	2 580	2 833	3 993	3 450	3 417	2 810	1 726	..	1 705	1 844	2 081	2 743
Transport equipment	548	814	796	1 038	766	944	897	576	519	662	695	840	877
4. and 9. Other	69	70	56	56	106	108	54	97	101	108	67	22	27
Total	7 367	9 633	9 983	14 019	15 064	15 757	13 334	12 154	11 996	12 164	11 750	12 603	13 154
Exports													
0. and 1. Food, drink and tobacco	618	607	687	720	1 023	1 157	1 147	1 152	1 084	975	916	994	1 046
of which: Live animals and meat	261	267	313	300	352	629	431	371	348	324	226	361	392
Cereals and cereal preparations	103	86	80	23	108	152	113	264	205	179	242	110	82
2. Raw materials	429	510	451	619	665	554	497	467	482	421	399	563	684
of which: Wood	248	315	265	318	368	293	251	240	241	186	172	248	301
5. Chemicals	353	331	469	636	1 010	1 377	1 073	960	995	1 190	1 199	1 291	1 156
6. Semi-manufactures	1 337	1 204	1 259	1 606	1 994	2 414	2 251	2 320	2 342	2 359	2 272	3 015	3 601
7. and 8. Finished manufactures	2 077	2 409	2 598	2 939	3 996	5 162	5 043	4 732	6 011	5 368	5 284	5 301	5 825
of which: Base metals	603	492	497	606	697	700	662	778	884	954	835	351	808
Machinery	802	1 000	1 030	1 329	1 656	2 117	2 147	1 148	1 146	1 135	1 310	1 321	2 603
Ships	287	415	421	252	317	310	323	339	503	819	497	303	472
3., 4. and 9. Other	64	195	204	274	289	265	230	282	399	329	228	262	285
Total	4 878	5 256	5 668	6 794	8 977	10 929	10 241	9 913	11 313	10 642	10 298	11 426	12 597

1. At statistical exchange rates before 1987. From 1987 onwards, at current exchange rate.
Source: Direct communication to the OECD.

Table L. Imports and exports by area[1]
Millions of US dollars

	1978	1979	1980	1981	1982	1983	1984	1985	1986	1987	1988[1]
							Imports,cif				
OECD countries	5 890	8 530	7 951	8 395	6 832	5 613	5 360	5 643	5 698	7 240	7 334
EEC	3 829	5 794	5 219	5 588	4 486	3 691	3 567	3 694	3 860	5 039	5 093
Italy	827	1 146	1 117	1 291	1 023	980	964	1 028	967	1 294	1 373
Germany	1 801	2 888	2 500	2 243	1 858	1 624	1 578	1 587	1 717	2 303	2 242
United States	615	1 059	1 015	957	846	775	620	778	673	716	725
Other	1 446	1 677	1 717	1 850	1 500	1 147	405	1 171	1 165	1 485	1 516
Centrally planned economies[2]	2 498	3 566	4 535	4 961	4 621	4 491	3 925	3 926	3 838	3 801	3 664
of which: USSR	1 375	1 793	2 698	2 966	2 737	2 463	1 964	1 977	1 874	1 926	1 809
Developing countries:	1 595	1 923	2 578	2 401	1 881	2 050	2 711	2 594	2 214	1 562	2 098
In Africa	397	570	936	1 126	833	187	168	141	182	154	576
In America	222	308	468	357	221	182	184	196	346	274	328
In Far-East	440	185	247	252	350	929	1 127	1 383	837	648	425
In Middle-East	536	860	927	666	477	752	1 232	874	848	485	769
In Europe								1.5	1.1	0.7	0.1
Total	9 983	14 019	15 064	15 757	13 334	12 154	11 996	12 163	11 750	12 603	13 096
							Exports,fob				
OECD countries	2 437	2 988	3 348	3 501	2 883	3 307	3 746	3 735	3 749	5 726	6 625
EEC	1 305	2 083	2 368	2 531	2 091	2 357	2 639	2 617	2 600	3 980	4 766
Italy	531	716	833	1 012	781	806	841	977	909	1 490	1 930
Germany	472	739	778	867	720	807	892	871	889	1 330	1 467
United States	371	373	393	387	311	346	432	463	565	733	760
Other	761	532	587	583	481	604	674	655	584	1 013	1 093
Centrally planned economies[2]	2 180	2 747	4 149	5 433	5 228	4 630	4 820	5 388	5 016	4 040	4 153
of which: USSR	1 394	1 401	2 489	3 644	3 424	2 699	2 797	3 397	3 122	2 222	2 304
Developing countries:	1 051	1 059	1 480	1 995	2 130	1 976	1 682	1 519	1 533	1 659	1 761
In Europe	3	4	5	4	4	8	4.6	9.3	6.8	6.8	3.8
In Africa	467	543	735	876	883	310	213	230	144	153	683
In America	47	27	57	74	65	62	85	194	154	161	152
In Far-East	300	128	206	311	293	984	904	672	649	510	335
In Middle-East	234	357	477	730	885	612	475	414	579	828	586
Total	5 668	6 794	8 977	10 929	10 241	9 913	10 248	10 642	10 298	11 425	12 539

1. At statistical exchange rates before 1987. From 1987 onwards, at current exchange rate.
2. Countries of Mutual Economic Assistance (CMEA), P.R. of China, and Albania.
Source: Direct communication to the OECD.

Table M. Balance of payments[1]
Millions of US dollars

	1979	1980	1981[2]	1982	1983	1984	1985	1986	1987	1988	1989
Trade balance	-7 225	-6 086	-4 828	-3 093	-2 240	-1 739	-1 601	-2 012	-1 178	-550	-1 442
Exports, fob	6 794	8 978	10 929	10 241	9 914	10 254	10 622	11 084	11 425	12 779	13 560
Imports, cif	-14 019	-15 064	-15 757	-13 334	-12 154	-11 993	-12 223	-13 096	-12 603	-13 329	-15 002
Services and transfers, net	3 564	3 795	4 078	2 629	2 514	2 243	2 434	271	2 426	3 037	3 859
Transportation	731	832	1 044	906	795	750	922	-1 749	1 030	950	850
Foreign travel	1 028	1 515	1 853	1 415	862	998	954	1 205	1 578	1 867	1 937
Investment income	-633	-1 084	-1 710	-1 773	-1 532	-1 638	-1 664	-1 749	-1 710	117	139
Private transfers and workers' remittances	1 710	1 539	2 042	1 268	1 167	1 789	1 651	1 636	998	1 438	1 487
Other services	728	993	849	813	1 222	344	571	928	530	-1 335	-554
Current Balance	-3 661	-2 291	-750	-464	274	504	833	-1 741	1 248	2 487	2 417
Long-term capital, net	1 590	2 281	1 458	479	1 363	-101	11	-1 677	-1 397	-1 163	-974
Loans received	1 740	2 516	1 708	679	1 519	1	100	-1 459	-1 178	-516	-801
Loans extended	-150	-235	-250	-200	-156	-102	-89	-218	-219	-647	-173
Short-term capital, net	283	739	261	-506	-647	-96	-36	350	-65	-267	-237
Bilateral balances (-: capital outflow)	-664	354	-770	-805	244	442	-434	-900	-131	65	-416
Errors and omissions	-153	-484	-79	284	-1 344	-213	-166	1 593	-729	316	1 858
Reserve movements (+: increase)	-1 277	599	120	-1 012	-110	536	208	466	-1 074	1 434	3 251

1. At statistical exchange rates until 1984. Statistical rates for 1983 and 1984 were, respectively, $1 = 63.40 dinars and $1 = 124.80 dinars. From 1987 onwards, at current exchange rates.
2. Trade figures in this table differ from those in tables K and L. In the above table the statistical exchange rate for 1981 used by the authorities is $1=41,80 dinars and in the latter tables it is $1=27.30 dinars.
Sources: IMF, Balance of payments Yearbook, and direct communication to the OECD.

BASIC STATISTICS

BASIC STATISTICS:

INTERNATIONAL COMPARISONS

	Units	Reference period[1]	Australia	Austria
Population				
Total	Thousands	1987	16 249	7 575
Inhabitants per sq.km	Number		2	90
Net average annual increase over previous 10 years	%		1.4	0.0
Employment				
Total civilian employment (TCE)[2]	Thousands	1987	7 079	32 997
of which: Agriculture	% of TCE		5.8	8.6
Industry	% of TCE		26.6	37.7
Services	% of TCE		67.6	53.7
Gross domestic product (GDP)				
At current prices and current exchange rates	Billion US$	1987	193.7	117.2
Per capita	US$		11 919	15 470
At current prices using current PPP's[3]	Billion US$	1987	204.9	88.4
Per capita	US$		12 612	11 664
Average annual volume growth over previous 5 years . . .	%	1987	3.7	1.8
Gross fixed capital formation (GFCF)	% of GDP	1987	23.8	22.6
of which: Machinery and equipment	% of GDP		11.5 (86)	9.7
Residential construction	% of GDP		4.7 (86)	4.6 (86)
Average annual volume growth over previous 5 years . . .	%	1987	1.7	2.3
Gross saving ratio[4]	% of GDP	1987	20.3	24.1
General government				
Current expenditure on goods and services	% of GDP	1987	18.2	19.0
Current disbursements[5]	% of GDP	1987	35.0 (86)	46.6 (86)
Current receipts	% of GDP	1987	34.7 (86)	47.9 (86)
Net official development assistance	% of GNP	1987	0.33	0.17
Indicators of living standards				
Private consumption per capita using current PPP's[3] . . .	US$	1987	7 389	6 535
Passenger cars, per 1 000 inhabitants	Number	1985	. .	306 (81)
Telephones, per 1 000 inhabitants	Number	1985	540 (83)	460 (83)
Television sets, per 1 000 inhabitants	Number	1985	. .	300 (81)
Doctors, per 1 000 inhabitants	Number	1985	. .	1.7 (82)
Infant mortality per 1 000 live births	Number	1985	9.2 (84)	11.0
Wages and prices (average annual increase over previous 5 years)				
Wages (earnings or rates according to availability)	%	1987	5.7	4.9
Consumer prices	%	1987	7.0	3.0
Foreign trade				
Exports of goods, fob*	Million US$	1987	26 484	27 084
as % of GDP	%		13.6	23.0
average annual increase over previous 5 years	%		4.4	11.6
Imports of goods, cif*	Million US$	1987	26 964	32 580
as % of GDP	%		13.9	27.7
average annual increase over previous 5 years	%		2.8	10.8
Total official reserves[6]	Million SDR's	1987	6 441	6 049
As ratio of average monthly imports of goods	Ratio		3.4	2.6

* At current prices and exchange rates.
1. Unless otherwise stated.
2. According to the definitions used in OECD *Labour force Statistics*.
3. PPP's = Purchasing Power Parities.
4. Gross saving = Gross national disposable income *minus* Private and Government consumption.
5. Current disbursements = Current expenditure on goods and services *plus* current transfers and payments of property income.
6. Gold included in reserves is valued at 35 SDR's per ounce. End of year.
7. Including Luxembourg.
8. Included in Belgium.
9. Including non-residential construction.

EMPLOYMENT OPPORTUNITIES

Economics and Statistics Department, OECD

The Economics and Statistics Department of the OECD offers challenging and rewarding opportunities to economists interested in applied policy analysis in an international environment. The Department's concerns extend across the entire field of economic policy analysis, both macroeconomic and microeconomic, and it is also responsible for the collection, processing and dissemination of a wide range of internationally consistent statistics. On the economic side, its main task is to provide, for discussion by committees of senior officials from Member countries, documents and papers dealing with current policy concerns. Within this programme of work, three major responsibilities are:

- To prepare regular surveys of the economies of individual Member countries;
- To issue full twice-yearly reviews of the economic situation and prospects of the OECD countries in the context of world economic trends;
- To analyse specific policy issues in a medium-term context for the OECD as a whole, and to a lesser extent for the non-OECD countries.

The documents prepared for these purposes, together with much of the Department's other economic work and its statistical output, appear in published form in the *OECD Economic Outlook, OECD Economic Surveys, OECD Economic Studies,* the Department's Working Paper series, and an extensive list of statistical publications.

The Department maintains a world econometric model, INTERLINK, which plays an important role in the preparation of the policy analyses and twice-yearly projections. The availability of extensive cross-country data bases and good computer resources facilitates comparative empirical analysis, much of which is incorporated into the model.

The Department is made up of about 90 professional economists and statisticians from a variety of backgrounds from all Member countries. Most projects are done by small teams and last from four to eighteen months. Within the Department, ideas and points of view are widely discussed; there is a lively professional interchange; and all professional staff have the opportunity to contribute actively to the programme of work.

Skills ESD is looking for

a) Solid competence in using the tools of both microeconomic and macroeconomic theory to answer policy questions. In our experience this requires the equivalent of a PhD in economics or substantial relevant professional experience to compensate for a lower degree.

b) Solid knowledge of economic statistics and quantitative methods; this includes how to identify data, estimate structural relationships, apply and interpret basic techniques of time series analysis, and test hypotheses. It is essential to be able to interpret results sensibly in an economic policy context.

c) A keen interest in and knowledge of policy issues, economic developments and their political/social contexts.

d) Interest and experience in analysing questions posed by policy-makers and presenting the results to them effectively and judiciously. Thus, work experience in government agencies or policy research institutions is an advantage.

e) The ability to write clearly, effectively, and to the point. The OECD is a bilingual organisation with French and English as the official languages. Candidates must have excellent knowledge of one of these languages, and some knowledge of the other. Knowledge of other languages might also be an advantage for certain posts.

f) For some posts, expertise in a particular area may be important, but a successful candidate can expect to be asked to contribute in a broader range of topics relevant to the work of the Department. Thus, except in rare cases, the Department does not recruit narrow specialists.

g) The Department works on a tight time schedule and strict deadlines. Moreover, much of the work in the Department is carried out in small groups of economists. Thus, the ability to work with other economists from a variety of professional backgrounds, and to produce work on time is important.

General Information

The salary for recruits depends on educational and professional background but positions carry a basic salary from FF 232 476 or FF 286 848 for Administrators (economists) and from FF 334 584 for Principal Administrators (senior economists). This may be supplemented by expatriation and/or family allowances, depending on nationality, residence and family situation. Initial appointments are for a fixed term of two to three years.

Vacancies are open to candidates from OECD Member countries. The Organisation seeks to maintain an appropriate balance between female and male staff and among nationals from Member countries.

For further information on employment opportunities in the Economics and Statistics Department, contact:

Executive Assistant
Economics and Statistics Department
OECD
2, rue André-Pascal
75775 PARIS CEDEX 16
FRANCE

Applications citing "ECSUR", together with a detailed curriculum vitae in English or French, should be sent to:

Head of Personnel
OECD
2, rue André-Pascal
75775 PARIS CEDEX 16
FRANCE

WHERE TO OBTAIN OECD PUBLICATIONS
OÙ OBTENIR LES PUBLICATIONS DE L'OCDE

Argentina – Argentine
Carlos Hirsch S.R.L.
Galeria Güemes, Florida 165, 4° Piso
1333 Buenos Aires
Tel. 30.7122, 331.1787 y 331.2391
Telegram: Hirsch-Baires
Telex: 21112 UAPE-AR. Ref. s/2901
Telefax:(1)331-1787

Australia – Australie
D.A. Book (Aust.) Pty. Ltd.
648 Whitehorse Road (P.O. Box 163)
Vic. 3132   Tel. (03)873.4411
Telex: AA37911 DA BOOK
Telefax: (03)873.5679

Austria – Autriche
OECD Publications and Information Centre
4 Simrockstrasse
5300 Bonn (Germany) Tel. (0228)21.60.45
Telex: 8 86300 Bonn
Telefax: (0228)26.11.04

Gerold & Co.
Graben 31
Wien I   Tel. (0222)533.50.14

Belgium – Belgique
Jean De Lannoy
Avenue du Roi 202
B-1060 Bruxelles
Tel. (02)538.51.69/538.08.41
Telex: 63220 Telefax: (02)538.08.41

Canada
Renouf Publishing Company Ltd.
1294 Algoma Road
Ottawa, Ont. K1B 3W8 Tel. (613)741.4333
Telex: 053-4783 Telefax: (613)741.5439
Stores:
61 Sparks Street
Ottawa, Ont. K1P 5R1 Tel. (613)238.8985
211 Yonge Street
Toronto, Ont. M5B 1M4 Tel. (416)363.3171
Federal Publications
165 University Avenue
Toronto, ON M5H 3B9 Tel. (416)581.1552
Telefax: (416)581.1743
Les Publications Fédérales
1185 rue de l'Université
Montréal, PQ H3B 1R7 Tel.(514)954–1633
Les Éditions La Liberté Inc.
3020 Chemin Sainte-Foy
Sainte-Foy, P.Q. G1X 3V6
Tel. (418)658.3763
Telefax: (418)658.3763

Denmark – Danemark
Munksgaard Export and Subscription Service
35, Nørre Søgade, P.O. Box 2148
DK-1016 København K
Tel. (45 33)12.85.70
Telex: 19431 MUNKS DK
Telefax: (45 33)12.93.87

Finland – Finlande
Akateeminen Kirjakauppa
Keskuskatu 1, P.O. Box 128
00100 Helsinki   Tel. (358 0)12141
Telex: 125080 Telefax: (358 0)121.4441

France
OECD/OCDE
Mail Orders/Commandes par correspon-
dance:
2 rue André-Pascal
75775 Paris Cedex 16   Tel. (1)45.24.82.00
Bookshop/Librairie:
33, rue Octave-Feuillet
75016 Paris   Tel. (1)45.24.81.67
                            (1)45.24.81.81
Telex: 620 160 OCDE
Telefax: (33–1)45.24.85.00
Librairie de l'Université
12a, rue Nazareth
13602 Aix-en-Provence   Tel. 42.26.18.08

Germany – Allemagne
OECD Publications and Information Centre
4 Simrockstrasse
5300 Bonn   Tel. (0228)21.60.45
Telex: 8 86300 Bonn
          Telefax: (0228)26.11.04

Greece – Grèce
Librairie Kauffmann
28 rue du Stade
105 64 Athens   Tel. 322.21.60
Telex: 218187 LIKA Gr

Hong Kong
Swindon Book Co. Ltd
13–15 Lock Road
Kowloon, Hong Kong   Tel. 366.80.31
Telex: 50.441 SWIN HX
Telefax: 739.49.75

Iceland – Islande
Mál Mog Menning
Laugavegi 18, Postholf 392
121 Reykjavik   Tel. 15199/24240

India – Inde
Oxford Book and Stationery Co.
Scindia House
New Delhi 110001   Tel. 331.5896/5308
Telex: 31 61990 AM IN
Telefax: (11)332.5993
17 Park Street
Calcutta 700016   Tel. 240832

Indonesia – Indonésie
Pdii-Lipi
P.O. Box 269/JKSMG/88
Jakarta12790   Tel. 583467
Telex: 62 875

Ireland – Irlande
TDC Publishers – Library Suppliers
12 North Frederick Street
Dublin 1   Tel. 744835/749677
Telex: 33530 TDCP EI Telefax : 748416

Italy – Italie
Libreria Commissionaria Sansoni
Via Benedetto Fortini, 120/10
Casella Post. 552
50125 Firenze   Tel. (055)645415
Telex: 570466 Telefax: (39.55)641257
Via Bartolini 29
20155 Milano   Tel. 365083
La diffusione delle pubblicazioni OCSE viene
assicurata dalle principali librerie ed anche
da:
Editrice e Libreria Herder
Piazza Montecitorio 120
00186 Roma   Tel. 679.4628
Telex: NATEL I 621427
Libreria Hoepli
Via Hoepli 5
20121 Milano   Tel. 865446
Telex: 31.33.95 Telefax: (39.2)805.2886
Libreria Scientifica
Dott. Lucio de Biasio "Aeiou"
Via Meravigli 16
20123 Milano   Tel. 807679
Telefax: 800175

Japan– Japon
OECD Publications and Information Centre
Landic Akasaka Building
2–3–4 Akasaka, Minato-ku
Tokyo 107   Tel. 586.2016
Telefax: (81.3)584.7929

Korea – Corée
Kyobo Book Centre Co. Ltd.
P.O. Box 1658, Kwang Hwa Moon
Seoul   Tel. (REP)730.78.91
Telefax: 735.0030

Malaysia/Singapore –
Malaisie/Singapour
University of Malaya Co-operative Bookshop
Ltd.
P.O. Box 1127, Jalan Pantai Baru 59100
Kuala Lumpur
Malaysia   Tel. 756.5000/756.5425
Telefax: 757.3661
Information Publications Pte. Ltd.
Pei-Fu Industrial Building
24 New Industrial Road No. 02–06
Singapore 1953   Tel. 283.1786/283.1798
Telefax: 284.8875

Netherlands – Pays-Bas
SDU Uitgeverij
Christoffel Plantijnstraat 2
Postbus 20014
2500 EA's-Gravenhage Tel. (070)78.99.11
Voor bestellingen: Tel. (070)78.98.80
Telex: 32486 stdru Telefax: (070)47.63.51

New Zealand –Nouvelle-Zélande
Government Printing Office
Customer Services
P.O. Box 12–411
Freepost 10–050
Thorndon, Wellington
Tel. 0800 733–406   Telefax: 04 499–1733

Norway – Norvège
Narvesen Info Center – NIC
Bertrand Narvesens vei 2
P.O. Box 6125 Etterstad
0602 Oslo 6
Tel. (02)67.83.10/(02)68.40.20
Telex: 79668 NIC N Telefax: (02)68.19.01

Pakistan
Mirza Book Agency
65 Shahrah Quaid-E-Azam
Lahore 3   Tel. 66839
Telex: 44886 UBL PK. Attn: MIRZA BK

Portugal
Livraria Portugal
Rua do Carmo 70–74
1117 Lisboa Codex   Tel. 347.49.82/3/4/5

Singapore/Malaysia
Singapour/Malaisie
See "Malaysia/Singapore"
Voir "Malaisie/Singapour"

Spain – Espagne
Mundi-Prensa Libros S.A.
Castello 37, Apartado 1223
Madrid 28001   Tel. (91) 431.33.99
Telex: 49370 MPLI Telefax: 575.39.98
Libreria Internacional AEDOS
Consejo de Ciento 391
08009 –Barcelona   Tel. (93) 301–86–15
Telefax: 575.39.98

Sweden – Suède
Fritzes Fackboksföretaget
Box 16356, S 103 27 STH
Regeringsgatan 12
DS Stockholm   Tel. (08)23.89.00
Telex: 12387 Telefax: (08)20.50.21
Subscription Agency/Abonnements:
Wennergren-Williams AB
Box 30004
104 25 Stockholm   Tel. (08)54.12.00
Telex: 19937 Telefax: (08)50.82.86

Switzerland – Suisse
OECD Publications and Information Centre
4 Simrockstrasse
5300 Bonn (Germany) Tel. (0228)21.60.45
Telex: 8 86300 Bonn
Telefax: (0228)26.11.04
Librairie Payot
6 rue Grenus
1211 Genève 11   Tel. (022)731.89.50
Telex: 28356
Maditec S.A.
Ch. des Palettes 4
1020 Renens/Lausanne Tel. (021)635.08.65
Telefax: (021)635.07.80
United Nations Bookshop/Librairie des Na-
tions-Unies
Palais des Nations
1211 Genève 10
Tel. (022)734.60.11 (ext. 48.72)
Telex: 289696 (Attn: Sales)
Telefax: (022)733.98.79

Taïwan – Formose
Good Faith Worldwide Int'l. Co. Ltd.
9th Floor, No. 118, Sec. 2
Chung Hsiao E. Road
Taipei   Tel. 391.7396/391.7397
Telefax: (02) 394.9176

Thailand – Thalande
Suksit Siam Co. Ltd.
1715 Rama IV Road, Samyan
Bangkok 5   Tel. 251.1630

Turkey – Turquie
Kültur Yayinlari Is-Türk Ltd. Sti.
Atatürk Bulvari No. 191/Kat. 21
Kavaklidere/Ankara   Tel. 25.07.60
Dolmabahce Cad. No. 29
Besiktas/Istanbul   Tel. 160.71.88
Telex: 43482B

United Kingdom – Royaume-Uni
H.M. Stationery Office
Gen. enquiries   Tel. (071) 873 0011
Postal orders only:
P.O. Box 276, London SW8 5DT
Personal Callers HMSO Bookshop
49 High Holborn, London WC1V 6HB
Telex: 297138 Telefax: 071.873.8463
Branches at: Belfast, Birmingham, Bristol,
Edinburgh, Manchester

United States – États-Unis
OECD Publications and Information Centre
2001 L Street N.W., Suite 700
Washington, D.C. 20036–4095
Tel. (202)785.6323
Telex: 440245 WASHINGTON D.C.
Telefax: (202)785.0350

Venezuela
Libreria del Este
Avda F. Miranda 52, Aptdo. 60337
Edificio Galipan
Caracas 106
Tel. 951.1705/951.2307/951.1297
Telegram: Libreste Caracas

Yugoslavia – Yougoslavie
Jugoslovenska Knjiga
Knez Mihajlova 2, P.O. Box 36
Beograd   Tel. 621.992
Telex: 12466 jk bgd

Orders and inquiries from countries where
Distributors have not yet been appointed
should be sent to: OECD Publications
Service, 2 rue André-Pascal, 75775 Paris
Cedex 16.
Les commandes provenant de pays où
l'OCDE n'a pas encore désigné de dis-
tributeur devraient être adressées à : OCDE,
Service des Publications, 2, rue André-
Pascal, 75775 Paris Cedex 16.

DATE DUE			

Organization   133723